early america and the book of mormon

early america and the Book of mormon

A PHOTOGRAPHIC ESSAY OF ANCIENT AMERICA

by Dr. Paul R. Cheesman
Director, Book of Mormon Institute
Brigham Young University

Deseret Book Company
Salt Lake City, Utah
1972

Library of Congress Catalog Card No. 72-76069

ISBN No. 87747-470-2

Copyright © 1972
by
DESERET BOOK COMPANY

PREFACE

Some travelers are startled to see the magnificent grandeur of the ruins of ancient America, and frankly, quite surprised to find that they compare favorably with the great cultures of ancient Rome and Greece.

As the author viewed these ancient structures in Central and South America over the past twenty years, he was filled with awe and wonder at the engineering and artistic accomplishments of the Americans before Columbus.

This book is an attempt to give the reader a view of some of the more outstanding ruins, including photographs that the author has taken on numerous research trips to these areas.

It is hoped that if the reader chooses to travel to these countries, this book will serve as enrichment material during his journey.

Dedicated to my wife, Millie, who has helped with the editing of this manuscript and has accompanied me on several research trips to Mexico, Central America, and South America. Her inspiring cooperation has been most needed and appreciated.

CONTENTS

Preface	v	Tula	49
Introduction	ix	Uxmal	51
The Time Scale	x	Xlapak	55
The Book of Mormon	xii	Zaculeu	57
Map of Central and South America	xiv	Xochicalco	59
Olmec Culture	xviii	Yagul	61
Maya Culture	xix	South America	63
Toltec Culture	xxi	Peru	65
Mixtec Culture	xxiii	The Incas	70
Zapotec Culture	xxiv	Mochica Culture	71
Aztec Culture	xxv	Chavin Culture	72
		Chancay Culture	73
Chichen Itza	1	Chimu Culture	74
Copan	5	Nasca Culture	75
Cuicuilco	7	Cajamarquilla	77
Dzibilchaltun	9	Chan Chan	79
Kaminaljuyu	11	Machu Picchu	81
Kabah	13	Cuzco	83
La Venta	15	Pachacamac	85
Labna	17	Paracas	87
Mitla	19	Sacsahuaman	89
Monte Alban	21	Tiahuanaco	91
Palenque	25	People and Culture	93
Cholula	27	Metallurgy	95
San Francisco	29	Jewelry	97
Sayil	31	Pottery	99
El Tajin	33	Trepanning	101
Tenayuca	35	Quipu	103
Tenochtitlan	37	Petroglyphs	105
Teotihuacan	39	Summary and Conclusions	106
Tikal	43	Pronunciation guide	108
Tzintzuntzan	47	Glossary	109

INTRODUCTION

The first inhabitants of the New World were the nomadic tribes of hunters and gatherers of plants. The beginning of human life on the American continent has been given various dates. It is sufficient for this treatment to say that the Archaic period would include these first inhabitants down to the time of the first farmers and into the examples of craftsmanship that started about 1000 B.C.

The pre-Classic period is divided into early, middle, and late periods, as shown on the chart. These were the early farmers who developed the numerous crops that became great sources of food. Although domestication of animals was a problem, the farmers were able to use irrigation and to produce an enormous variety of products, among which maize seems to be the most prominent.

The Classic period relates to those civilizations which enjoyed an aesthetic, architectural, and intellectual flowering.

A series of disturbances brought the Classic period to an end. The post-Classic period, which commenced in an atmosphere of confusion and lasted until the conquest, represents the cultures that developed following the collapse of the Classic period civilization. The various peoples were attempting to build a new society over the breakdown of an old order by regrouping and forming new and militaristic states.

The Time Scale

For the purpose of identifying the ancient cultures of the New World, the writer wishes to establish the following periods:

Post-Classic	Late	A.D. 1520
		A.D. 1200
	Early	A.D. 1600
		A.D. 900
Classic	Late	A.D. 900-600
	Early	A.D. 500-300
Pre-Classic	Late	A.D. 300-300 B.C.
	Middle	500-1000 B.C.
	Early	1000-2000 B.C.
Archaic		3000 B.C. and earlier

The times stipulated are approximate, but the major groupings are accepted by qualified authorities in the field. Some experts, however, disagree on the subtitle classifications, and the writer assumes the responsibility for the groupings as listed, basing these time periods on a comparison of several accepted references.

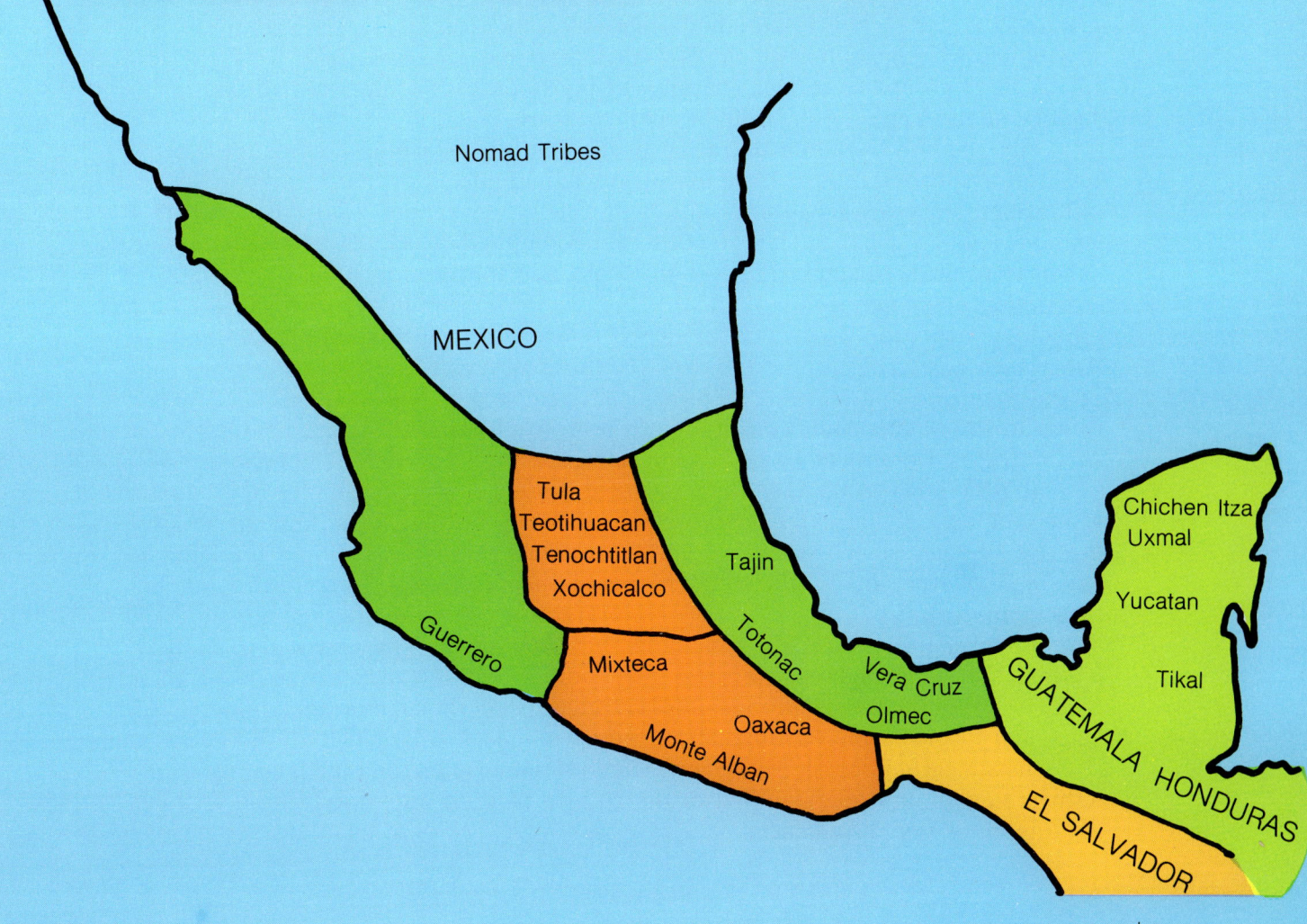

xi

THE BOOK OF MORMON

The Book of Mormon is a religious history of some of the ancestors of the American Indian and an epic that records the divisions of a people into three groups: the Lehi colony, which divided into the Nephites and Lamanites; the Mulekites, who merged with the Nephites; and the Jaredites, who were the first of the three groups to arrive. The bulk of the Book of Mormon is made up of the history of the Nephite-Lamanite-Mulekite culture.

The Nephite-Lamanite narrative in the Book of Mormon commenced in 600 B.C. and terminated in A.D. 421. This chronicle is reported primarily by two writers—Mormon and his son Moroni—although nine other writers contributed. Mormon and Moroni abridged ancient records and compiled a set of metal plates that, when translated, became 522 pages in length and the present Book of Mormon.

Modern science divided into the fields of anthropology, archaeology, and ethnology has provided much evidence concerning the ancient inhabitants of America. Many terms are used to describe these natives who lived prior to the time of the Spanish conquerors. The term used here will be "pre-Columbian," which refers to the groups found on the North and South American continents prior to the arrival of Columbus.

In attempting to recreate the story of the pre-Columbian peoples of America, a methodology of various disciplines was utilized. Part of these findings involve the use of manuscripts prepared by the natives themselves. Some hieroglyphs and records were made anciently. Many of these writings were destroyed, but three manuscripts or codices have been found thus far. Some hieroglyphs on stone and other materials are also available but have not been translated. Natives learned the Spanish language after the conquest and translated some of their manuscripts and oral traditions into a tongue that the conquerors understood. One such record is the writings of an Indian named Ixtlilxochitl.

Certain early Spanish priests and scholars likewise learned the language of the natives to gain an understanding of the culture of their ancestors. These writings are known as the chronicles.

Artifacts from the material remains of these great ancient civilizations, such as potsherds, jewelry, clothing, metal objects, musical instruments, and surgical tools, have been assembled, correlated, compared, and dated to produce hypotheses concerning the pre-Columbian civilization. All of these investigations are part of a new science known as archaeology, which emerged at the turn of the century. Many mysteries still exist as attempts are made to determine the origin and environment of the early inhabitants of the American continent.

The Book of Mormon as a religious record of these people is an abridgment, and the authors recorded that they had written "an hundredth part" of what they could have written.

The contributions of the scientific world, as well as the religious and historical data provided in the Book of Mormon, reveal that prior to the arrival of the Spanish, the civilization of the American continent was fantastic. The people evidenced superb architectural achievements, agricultural irrigation systems, masterful engineering accomplishments, and well-planned civic, political, and religious organizations. In most every facet of living the civilization of these ancient ancestors of the American Indian compared favorably with the majesty and greatness of Rome and Greece.

Many parallels can be made with the Old and the New Worlds, with transoceanic travel emerging as a definite possibility.

As the reader studies photographs and descriptions of the places visited by the author, and shown in the following pages, it is the writer's hope that he might develop a deep appreciation for the advanced civilization that once existed here. The author also suggests that a God who is not a respector of persons would visit, instruct, and leave a record of his dealings with the millions of people of this new world as well as the old. Translations of ancient Indian histories, as well as the Book of Mormon, bear this out. Many Indian traditions reveal a knowledge of the flood, the ark, the dividing of the waters, and other biblical happenings, all told to the Spaniards when they arrived in the New World.

MAP OF CENTRAL AND SOUTH AMERICA

One of the two focal points of the ancient civilizations of the American Indian is found in the countries now known as Mexico, Guatemala, Honduras, and Salvador; a modern terminology for this area is Mesoamerica. The other center is the narrow coastal region and highlands of the Middle Andes, covering the greater part of modern Peru, part of Equador, and Bolivia. While the Andean cities were built apparently to be lived in and to give shelter, many structures of Mesoamerica were ceremonial centers. The soil on which the Central American native lived was more fertile than coastal Peru, and therefore a greater variety of plants could be cultivated, the climate was milder, and the forests were rich in game.

The Inca empire developed in the central highlands of Peru, with its capital city in Cuzco. A well-balanced social order characterized this tremendous civilization, with an influential nobility and a strong religion. A network of roads kept communications open to all surrounding cities in a surprisingly efficient manner.

This photographic study will treat both areas and will start with the ruins of Mesoamerica. Involved in the time scale were several cultures in different areas, and some overlapped in the same areas. A discussion follows of six major Mesoamerican cultures: Olmec, Maya, Toltec, Mixtec, Zapotec, and Aztec.

MAP OF CENTRAL AND SOUTH AMERICA

One of the two focal points of the ancient civilizations of the American Indian is found in the countries now known as Mexico, Guatemala, Honduras, and Salvador; a modern terminology for this area is Mesoamerica. The other center is the narrow coastal region and highlands of the Middle Andes, covering the greater part of modern Peru, part of Equador, and Bolivia. While the Andean cities were built apparently to be lived in and to give shelter, many structures of Mesoamerica were ceremonial centers. The soil on which the Central American native lived was more fertile than coastal Peru, and therefore a greater variety of plants could be cultivated, the climate was milder, and the forests were rich in game.

The Inca empire developed in the central highlands of Peru, with its capital city in Cuzco. A well-balanced social order characterized this tremendous civilization, with an influential nobility and a strong religion. A network of roads kept communications open to all surrounding cities in a surprisingly efficient manner.

This photographic study will treat both areas and will start with the ruins of Mesoamerica. Involved in the time scale were several cultures in different areas, and some overlapped in the same areas. A discussion follows of six major Mesoamerican cultures: Olmec, Maya, Toltec, Mixtec, Zapotec, and Aztec.

Artifacts from the material remains of these great ancient civilizations, such as potsherds, jewelry, clothing, metal objects, musical instruments, and surgical tools, have been assembled, correlated, compared, and dated to produce hypotheses concerning the pre-Columbian civilization. All of these investigations are part of a new science known as archaeology, which emerged at the turn of the century. Many mysteries still exist as attempts are made to determine the origin and environment of the early inhabitants of the American continent.

The Book of Mormon as a religious record of these people is an abridgment, and the authors recorded that they had written "an hundredth part" of what they could have written.

The contributions of the scientific world, as well as the religious and historical data provided in the Book of Mormon, reveal that prior to the arrival of the Spanish, the civilization of the American continent was fantastic. The people evidenced superb architectural achievements, agricultural irrigation systems, masterful engineering accomplishments, and well-planned civic, political, and religious organizations. In most every facet of living the civilization of these ancient ancestors of the American Indian compared favorably with the majesty and greatness of Rome and Greece.

Many parallels can be made with the Old and the New Worlds, with transoceanic travel emerging as a definite possibility.

As the reader studies photographs and descriptions of the places visited by the author, and shown in the following pages, it is the writer's hope that he might develop a deep appreciation for the advanced civilization that once existed here. The author also suggests that a God who is not a respector of persons would visit, instruct, and leave a record of his dealings with the millions of people of this new world as well as the old. Translations of ancient Indian histories, as well as the Book of Mormon, bear this out. Many Indian traditions reveal a knowledge of the flood, the ark, the dividing of the waters, and other biblical happenings, all told to the Spaniards when they arrived in the New World.

central america

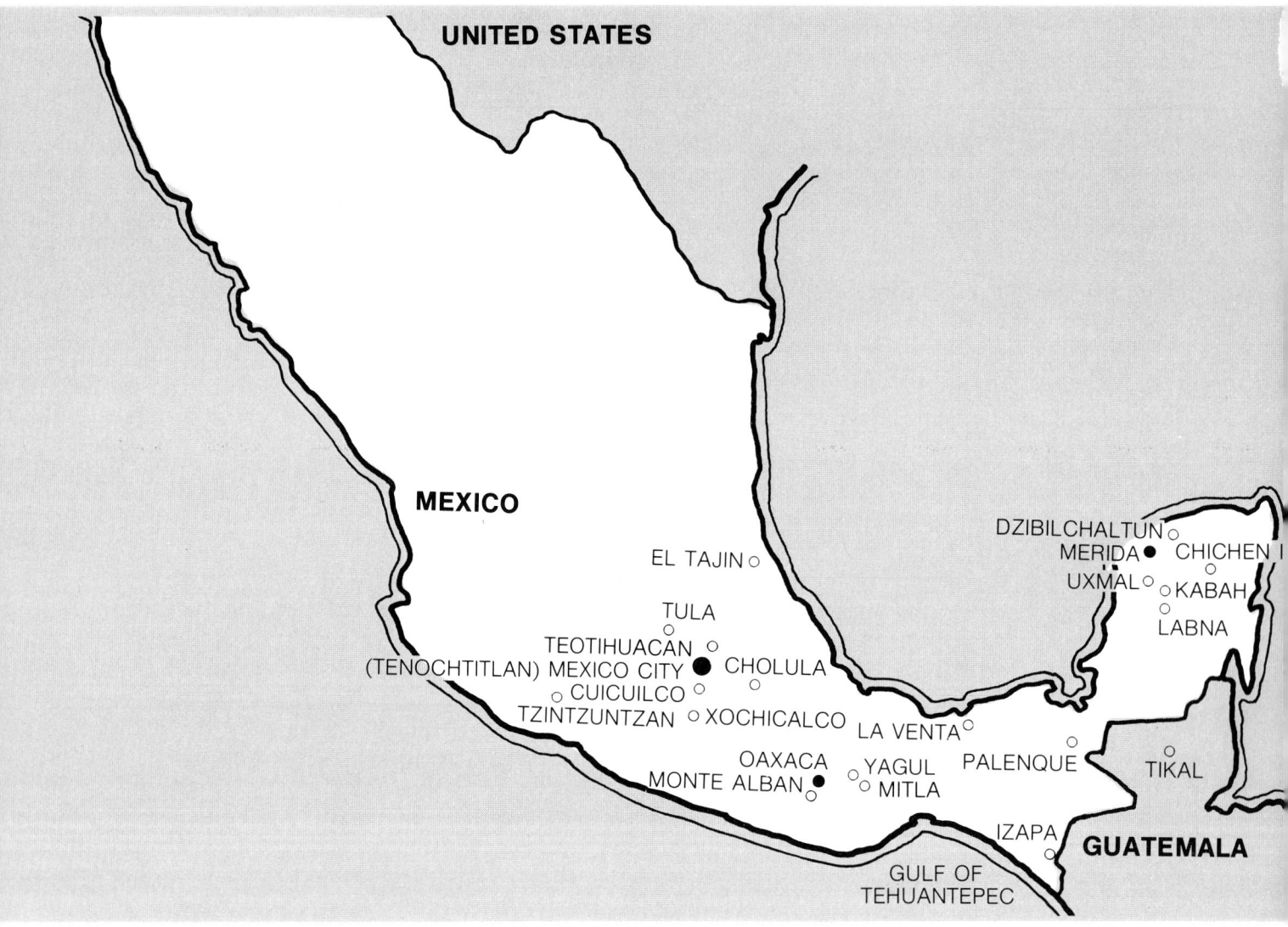

OLMEC CULTURE

Sometimes referred to as the La Venta development, the Olmec culture flourished near the southern part of Mexico in the areas known as Vera Cruz and Tabasco. Olmec is the name given by modern scholars to the people who created this marvelous culture in the middle pre-Classic period, with La Venta being the most important archaeological site of the Olmec people. The Olmec culture, which had its peak from approximately 1200 to 400 B.C., is often referred to as the mother culture of Middle America. At the present, numerous mysteries fog the history of the Olmecs. However, the Olmec culture was a golden one. One of the earliest civilizations—if not the earliest—to develop in southeastern Mexico, the Olmecs created a religious art of a high standard. Their religion was centered around a jaguar and the ceremonies of the priests.

Unique are the massive stone heads, more than six feet high, carved in extremely hard stone. These heads were made from basalt carved in a rounded fashion, and weighed up to twenty tons. Many heads look as if they have some kind of helmet on them. The source of the stone is not found in the immediate locale, and much mystery surrounds the method involved in transporting such large stones.

The Olmecs erected pyramids and stepped platforms, used as temples and altars. The La Venta hieroglyphs and calendar systems resemble those of the early Mayan culture. These people were the first to build large planned religious centers. Often included in the temple areas were sacrificial altars, stelae of various sizes, colossal stone carvings, sculptured panels, walls, and temple mounds. These sites were the centers of a strong religious cult.

The Olmecs were masters in art and carving. They have left behind an excellent display of sculptures in the round, terra-cotta, figurines, decorated pottery, a variety of masks, and jade statuettes. Their impressive art style is among the most exquisite that has appeared in Middle America. Olmecs freely diffused with their neighbors, leaving an indelible impression on all who were to come after them.

MAYA

The culture of the Maya civilization is thought by many to be supreme among the ancient ancestors of the American Indian. Hieroglyphic writings, in addition to achievements in astronomy and mathematics, have been responsible partly for this superior rating. The Mayan area is usually considered to be the jungle country lying north and northwest of Guatemala, the Peten district of Guatemala, and the adjoining parts of British Honduras and Mexico. The Maya culture is thought to have developed about 600 B.C. or earlier and to have begun to decline many years before the Spaniards arrived. The pulse of the Maya civilization lay in the cities of Copan, Chichen Itza, Uxmal, Tikal, Calakmul, and Coba (some think that these were probably not true cities with suburbs but rather religious centers inhabited by relatively few persons).

The Mayas used a calendar system thought by some to be more accurate that the Christian calendar in use at the time of Columbus. The centers abandoned by the Mayan people seem to indicate that they had a strong community sense and clean habits, and were deeply religious. They apparently possessed a passion for learning and building, as well as artistic skills. They elaborated on the inventions and ideas of previous Middle American cultures. Much of Mayan country is thick, tropical rain forest, difficult to clear for agriculture, and yet the people were able to build magnificent centers.

Their writing does not seem to be based on an alphabet; the glyphs represented ideas, words, and numbers. Their numbering system involved placing numbers one above another instead of side by side as we do. However, some scholars believe the Mayas developed a combination of ideographic and phonetic writing. Their artistic objects include stone mosaics, carvings in jade, paintings, and codices; metallurgy includes manufactured objects of gold and copper with alloys.

The basic method of planting entailed burning the plant overgrowth and planting the seeds. After two years of use the farmer moved on and the process was repeated.

Their principal crop was corn, and they were probably the best farmers for their time and region. Other crops included red and black beans, squash, cassava, tomatoes, chayote, bread nut, and sweet potato. Food was seasoned with spices, vanilla, and chili peppers.

Mayan life seems to have been influenced by religious systems with graded priesthood. The religion was highly organized, and the people practiced sacrifice of goods and animals. Religion appears to be the central, motivating influence in their lives. In certain aspects their religion was polytheistic, with most of the gods representing agricultural ideas; however, some have theorized these to be symbols of a monotheistic deity. The sacred book of the Quiche Maya, which was written in the Mayan language but used Spanish characters, asserts that of the several gods, Itzamna was the Lord of the Heavens. There is every indication that the ancients worshipped many gods but still believed in a single creator of the world. Their religious beliefs included a concept of immortality, baptism, and the basic idea of good and evil. Elaborate ceremonies practiced by the Mayas included fasting, prayers, exorcism, and abstinence, followed by the sacrificing of birds, animals, and humans.

The Mayan calendar commences on August 11, 3113 B.C., but as to what is the historical significance of this date, no one seems to know. One by one the keepers of the books died and entrusted their writings to successors, and during generations of war and struggle with the white man, comprehension of the existing writings and histories became imperfect. Many of the books that remained were burned by the conquerors.

At the present time it is estimated there are over two million Maya-speaking Indians living in Mesoamerica who are descendants of the ancient Maya. Most of these live in what we now call Guatemala.

Mayan history was thought to have existed first in the Guatemalan highlands and then been moved to the Peten area, where Tikal, the largest and perhaps the oldest city, was established. From here the culture spread southeast to Palenque, southwest to Copan, and later north to inhabit the Yucatan peninsula, where we now find the cities Chichen Itza and Uxmal.

It appears that Mayan cities were not laid out with planned streets and avenues, but rather the buildings were erected around courts and plazas that were the religious, governmental, and trading sectors of the city. The houses of the more important leaders were erected around this central grouping, while the other houses and farms of the common people reached farther out in every direction. The main building technique was the use of rubber masonry plastered with pulverized limestone cement, finished with a facing of carefully worked stone. This facing was sometimes embellished with painted stucco. The two distinguishing characteristics unique to Central America are the corbeled arch and the false facade at roof level.

The Mayas had a class system composed of slaves, lords, and royalty. At birth a person could be redeemed from slavery. A thief was made a slave to the person from whom he stole in order to pay for the article and then was released. Captives of war were made slaves. Slaves built the houses for the rich and tended their fields. Their social status was based on how near the central plaza they lived. However, these were probably not true cities with suburbs, but rather religious centers inhabited by relatively few.

The mode of dress was simple. Men wore wrapped clothlike arrangements around the loins; the rich wore highly decorated garments; and women wore long sacklike dresses.

Mayan men did not have mustaches or beards; mothers used hot cloths to burn the faces of their young sons and plucked out growing hairs. Many newborn babies had their heads tied between two flat boards, to produce a flattened head. In youth the children had their ears, nose, and lips pierced.

The Mayan civilization is considered by some to be the most enlightened and influential culture in all of Mesoamerica.

TOLTEC CULTURE

The Toltecs were a highly civilized people who made Tula their capital. According to Sahagun, they were skilled with their hands as craftsmen and feather workers. They were a wealthy people with no poor among them. This culture preceded the Aztec and followed the Teotihuacan, and existed in the early part of the post-Classic period starting about A.D. 900.

The Toltecs, forerunners of the high cultures of the Valley of Mexico, were masters of art, medicine, calendrics, engineering, and carving. They were intensely religious and steeped in rich pageantry. The laws were very strict but just and fair.

Because of civil strife and decay, their enemies forced them south, where they inhabited the central part of Mexico. It is thought that later they moved north and east, where they settled the area of Yucatan. Rampant civil strife was the eventual downfall of this once great nation. They were a very warlike race, having a catalytic effect on all of their neighbors both in culture and in politics.

Archaeologists have uncovered magnificent frescoes of jaguars and vultures feeding on human hearts on the walls of Tula's pyramids. Many sculptured items —both painted and unpainted—have been found.

That the Toltecs loved sports is evidenced by their ball courts and massive caryatids. Their cities had sunken plazas and courts, walls of carved serpents, many altars decorated with skull motifs, and images of the plumed Quetzalcoatl.

The Toltec peoples were the designers of the pyramid El Castillo (Temple of Kukulcan) in Chichen Itza. It is a gigantic structure of terraces that recede in size to form a 75-foot building. However, architecture was rather simple, giving way to plain design over rich extravagance. This culture seems to have been more interested in everyday life than in rich luxury. They did use colonnades (square and/or rounded) on a series of stone drums with backing walls. A variety of roofs were constructed, such as beam and mortar, thatched, or the Maya corbel vaulting. Vaulted roofs were constructed on long wooden lintels. Temples were rounded, and most buildings had wide doorways. Low relief sculptured paneling and balustrades were popular and featured the feathered serpent. Masonry walls are also common on Toltec buildings.

The Toltecs based their religion around Kukulcan. It is evident that when the Toltecs conquered the Mayas, the Mayas greatly influenced the Toltec religion through Mayan art, imagery, and ceremonies. The Maya priest helped in the design of Toltec temples. The high priest of Yucatan was supported by gifts from the people, and in turn he appointed all other priests. The lords' sons were trained with the priests in calendrics, religious ceremonies, prophecies, Maya writing, and cures for diseases. Most of the learning was abstracted from the Mayas into the Toltec culture.

MIXTEC CULTURE

The Mixtec culture geographically had far-reaching effects. It was partly responsible for the rise of Cholula, spreading over Middle America, south to Guatemala, and north to the Mississippi area. In time the Mixtecs took over the ruins of Monte Alban and Mitla, and Mitla eventually became the religious and political center for the Mixtec culture. Mixtec means "a dweller in the land of clouds." The Mixtecs came from the Oaxaca region about the ninth century A.D. and probably started their culture about a century before then. They had a loose form of government in which unity took second place. The expanding Mixtec kingdom was subdivided into chiefdoms, each ruled by a hereditary chief. Their society was divided into two classes: one comprised of the nobles, priests, merchants, and other high class people, and the other made up of craftsmen and peasants.

Mixtecs were sharp businessmen. Through war, which they loved, they conquered their neighbors and made extensive use of their resources. Well advanced in calendrics, astronomy, and writing, they used goat skins to make codices that told of their history, their religion, and their everyday life. They used carefully painted pictures to tell their story. Their religion included a host of gods—one for every occasion.

The temples and pyramids were constructed of simple design. However, they were highly garnished with decorative elements as stone mosaic in relief on painted backgrounds. Their sculpture is limited to seated male and female figures in green stone, representing the funerary position.

The Mixtecs' creative skills favor craftsmanship over artistry. Their craftsmanship is displayed in ceramics (bichrome pottery—vermillion, black, or dark maroon on white), engraving, metal work, key-pattern decoration, polychrome pottery, jars, tripods, and zoomorphic vessels (eagles and jaguars). Engraving is confined to jaguar bones with stellar motifs and inscriptions.

Their metallurgy was among the finest; jewelry was produced by the repousse methods, and the people wore pictoral plaques, nose ornaments, rings, and necklaces. Earrings were produced with refined execution and remarkable beauty. As goldsmiths they ranked supreme in Mexico.

ZAPOTEC CULTURE

Sometime during the second century B.C., the mighty Zapotec culture began to develop, which cultural influence would eventually range from the Gulf of Mexico to the shores of the Pacific Ocean. These people covered the high valleys of Oaxaca, Etla, Tlacolula, and Zimatlan. Here in the rifts of the mountain chains they built such great cities as Monte Alban and Mitla.

Like the Mayas and Aztecs, the Zapotecs had a vast knowledge of astronomy, calendrics, and glyphic writing, which they used for recording history and religion. They were highly influenced by the Olmecs and Mayas, and late in the tenth century elements from the Mixtecs were incorporated into their culture.

Art was an integral part of the Zapotec religion. A number of funerary urns in terra cotta have been discovered; the urns are molded in the shape of people with elaborate decorations, and feathered and ornamental motifs are common. The tomb walls are covered with carved relief panels or elaborate frescoes.

They were highly skilled with pottery, which comes in a myriad of sizes, shapes, and colors. They were masters in catching facial expressions.

The Zapotecs did not let the mountains hinder them in building huge pyramid-like temples, where the priests carried out their religious ceremonies. These people were brilliant engineers in scraping and leveling hills and erecting monuments. They used circular pillars, wide and numerous steps, and impressive bas-relief figures carved in large stone slabs.

Evidence so far indicates that they were a non-warring people. This is probably due to the fact that they lived very high in the mountains and were not readily accessible to conquering neighbors.

AZTEC CULTURE

The Aztec groups were less united than their contemporaries in the Incan empire of Peru. They were content to exist as several tribes and lacked a united central government, which was indigenous to their South American neighbors. The Aztec culture seems to be based on a deep theocratic philosophy. Their capital was the famous Tenochtitlan over which the present Mexico City has been built.

Aztec society began with the building of the city of Tenochtitlan, about A.D. 1300. The culture grew rapidly and encompassed the surrounding tribes and their neighbors. A military people, they were continually subjecting new peoples to their conquering rule and obtaining prisoners for sacrifice. Their young men were trained in special military colleges to become warriors.

Tenochtitlan was built on a lake. As the city expanded, the lake was filled in, but a network of canals connected the various parts of the city. The main building was the Great Pyramid, which was topped by two temples.

The Aztecs made great use of cut-stone blocks, volcanic rock, and unbaked clay in constructing their cities. Their craftsmanship is evident in ornate stone carvings, decorative buildings, iconographic signs, statues, and reliefs.

They were also great artisans and metal workers. Fine examples remain of their jewelry, jade carvings, pottery, paintings, murals, and statuary.

They developed a complex system of writing of which only numbers, dates, and names of months and gods can be translated. Drawings, paintings, and conventional signs were employed to represent ideas or motion.

The Aztec culture was a very religious one, with worship divided amongst a host of gods. Human sacrifice became ritualistic, and men, women, and children were all sacrificed to satisfy the jealousy of the gods. War captives often ended up on the sacrificial altar without their hearts, for the Aztecs believed the gods needed hearts and blood to live on.

One of the most noted monuments to the Aztec people is their calendar, which expresses in superior workmanship Aztec art, astronomy, and mathematics. It was started in 1427 and finished in 1479. On the edge are eight equidistant holes into which pegs were inserted so the stone could be used as a sun dial.

Temple of Kulkulcan, Chichen Itza

Chichén Itzá

Chichen Itza, an ancient city of considerable size, is seventy miles east of Merida in Yucatan. This great complex of buildings indicates the existence of at least two periods of development. One is late Classic from A.D. 650 to 900, and the other dates later during the Toltec period. However, some researchers believe it to have been populated as early as the fifth century A.D. Some of the buildings built during the earlier period were altered and used by the later inhabitants, while other dwellings were erected over old structures, and still others remain unchanged.

Chichen Itza is a synthesis of styles, combining the Mayan and Toltec religions and cultures. The temple and buildings appear to have been placed at random, and among the buildings is a sacred well called cenote, which was used for several purposes, including sacrificial offerings. Sometimes these sacrifices were human, along with jewelry, pottery, and other valuable possessions. Archaeological workers, in dredging this area, have found numerous ancient articles in this well.

Many of the buildings are built out of a pumice-type granite that possesses great acoustical qualities—in fact, in some locales one can hear an echo as many as fourteen times.

The Castillo or Temple of Kulkulcan

This ziggurat temple, located near the center of the complex of buildings in Chichen Itza, is perhaps the best known, most photographed pre-Columbian temple in Central America or Mexico.

Four stairways, with 91 steps on each side, lead to the top of the pyramid; the 364 steps plus the top step total 365, which is thought by some to represent the days of the year.

The small building atop the pyramid is believed to have been used for religious purposes. The entrance to this worship building is divided by two columns, representing a serpent's head facing down, thus making an entrance with three doorways.

The Temple of Kulkulcan in its present state was built over another temple that has been uncovered through tunneled excavation. The condition of the interior sanctuary seems to be in good condition and most of the building has been left intact.

A *chacmool*, an effigy or reclining figure, was found at the bottom of the main stairway. Inside and perhaps a part of the original structure is a room containing a red painted jaguar with the spots represented by jade discs.

The Caracol is one of the buildings situated somewhat at random amongst the complex of structures in Chichen Itza. The building, which has an interior spiral staircase called a "snail-shell stairway," appears to have been built in a series of succeeding cultural periods. The round tower is unique among ancient architectural styles, and the stairway leading to its top is barely wide enough for one person. Some have speculated that this dome-shaped tower could have been used for astronomical observations. Doors and windows were so constructed that the equinoxes and solstices were observed. The Mayan and Toltec civilizations who once used this structure and other adjacent buildings left abruptly and mysteriously. However, the contributions of the people who inhabited this area are numerous and the study of their civilization fascinating.

The ball court at Chichen Itza is thought to be the largest yet discovered. Associated with the ball court is the Temple of the Jaguars. The proximity of the temple to the ball court suggests that the game represented more than just a recreational event. The players are thought by some scholars to have been participants in a ritualistic religious ceremony. So serious were the implications of this game that legend and a few sculptured artifacts suggest the loser was decapitated.

The court measures 272 feet long and

The Caracol (Observatory), Chichen Itza

199 feet wide, and the walls are 27 feet high. At either end is a small temple, with the building to the north containing extensive bas-reliefs of Toltec life.

Two donut-like stone rings were placed midway on the upper part of the two walls of the court, with the object of the game being to knock a rubber ball through the hole in the ring. Spanish chroniclers tell us that hands could not be used to hit the ball, only the other portions of the body. Many ball courts similar to this appear throughout Mexico, so it was apparently a very popular ancient sport.

Temple of the Warriors, Chichen Itza

Ball court at Copan

copan

Copan is thought to be the second largest ancient metropolis in the southern half of the peninsula, and a great seat of learning for the ancient inhabitants.

The main structure, covering about 75 acres, is composed of the Acropolis and five adjoining plazas. At this spectacular Acropolis, an architectural complex of pyramids, terraces, and temples, we find the most complete inscriptions in Mayan hieroglyphics. Researchers believe that the important astronomical discovery of determining the exact length of intervals between eclipses was calibrated here. There were also great calculators and mathematicians who regulated the peoples' lives by the heavenly bodies.

Elaborately carved altars and monoliths (stelae) found in the plaza represent the efforts of the greatest artistic sculptors of their time. A superb hieroglyphic stairway, 33 feet wide and with 62 steps, contains between 1500 and 2000 individual glyphs.

Erosion from the river has exposed a vertical face 118 feet high and nearly 1000 feet long. Even earlier plaza floor levels and drains can be distinguished. Copan also claims the distinction of having the largest architectural cross-section in the world.

Stelae at Copan, Honduras

Most of the monuments in Copan, a city of temples and stairways, were built after a 20-year period, and each building is dated. This ancient city is also the home of many burial tombs and markers carved with the Mayan hieroglyphics. The founding of Copan is placed at A.D. 176, according to the Mayan glyphs.

The circular pyramid of Cuicuilco

cuicuilco

Agriculture and the art of pottery making and weaving laid the foundation for a high standard of culture in the pre-Classic era at Cuicuilco, Mexico. It is in Cuicuilco, to the south of the Valley of Mexico, that some of the first monuments on the American continent were erected.

The oldest one, basically in an oval form, was made entirely of earth. Later (sometime before the birth of Christ) the so-called Pyramid of Cuicuilco was built near the outskirts of Mexico City; it is actually a truncated cone 80 feet high and 389 feet in diameter, with the top being made of four sections connected by a ramp and stairway. Uncut stones were placed one on top of the other, with no cementing mortar. In its first phase the building was small and had only two sections, with others added later. As we see it today, it retains only a general resemblance to its original form, for it has not been possible to undertake an exact reconstruction. Atop the mound, the temple covered a square thatched-roof altar, of which little remains. Around the central building were other buildings of smaller dimensions, which were among the first of the ceremonial complexes that we shall find later in all the monumental cities.

By the time the Christian era was ushered in, a great catastrophe had annihilated the site of Cuicuilco. Small Xitle, a nearby volcano, insignificant in appearance, erupted and covered with lava not only the monuments of Cuicuilco, but also a vast region to the south and west of the Valley of Mexico, known today by the name of Pedregal (stony ground). At Copilco, a place near Cuicuilco, remains of settlements and burial grounds have been uncovered. Imprints of men and dogs show that these victims were probably caught by surprise in the volcanic flow. The findings indicate that these people cultivated maize, caught fish, kept dogs, and used quartz and obsidian arrowheads.

Dzibilchaltun

Close to the ocean, north of the city of Merida, Yucatan, Mexico, lie the ruins of Dzibilchaltun, covering more than twenty square miles. E. Wyllys Andrews began excavating the ruins, which may be the largest Mayan city, in about 1956. The levels of occupation indicate that the earliest habitation could have been near 2000 B.C., and it appears to have been continuously inhabited until the Spanish conquest.

Dzibilchaltun is believed to have been a trade center for a vast area, for discarded and broken pottery, in a sequence of ceramics covering several thousand years, has been found in the foundations and walls. Excavation of a large well or cenote in the center of the area has unearthed pottery from several phases of Mayan civilization, and the pottery is close to that of Oxhintok and Tzakol. Decorative motifs and murals in stucco adorn the walls. The city was built around plazas and patios, and stelae dot the city ruins.

Tradition has it that the city was submerged when the big lake of Boca Paila suddenly formed. The city, which was the center of a populous urban area in the Classic period, had sustained the longest known continuous habitation of any Mayan city (2000 to 3000 years). It was a main trade center of the entire area and possibly with cities of other empires.

At present Dzibilchaltun is undergoing excavation by Tulane University and the National Geographic Society.

Cenote at Dzibilchaltun

Prominent building at Dzibilchaltun, Yucatan

An undeveloped mound at Kaminaljuyu

kaminaljuyu

On the outskirts of Guatemala City lie some of the most interesting ruins of earlier times. The date of this civilization has been estimated at approximately 850 B.C. Several surrounding mounds, indicating buildings underneath, dot the landscape of this fertile valley. Many groups lived here, with each successive culture building over the previous one, and over 200 mounds have been counted.

A single stairway leads to each stage, at the top of which is a temple sanctuary, roofed either with thatch or flat beam and mortar construction. The absence of stone sculpture is noticeable. There is evidence that prominent people of the community were buried inside the temple buildings. The temple platforms seem to have been built to enclose the rulers' tomb, with successive burials being placed over the older ones. Rich offerings of jade, pearls, mica, and textiles surround the bodies of the dead, and more than one body was usually found in one area. The ceramics and jade date from 2000 to 1500 B.C., perhaps the oldest known in Central America.

Excavations allow the visitor to walk through narrow passageways to view some of the interiors by candlelight.

Kaminaljuyu means "Hills of the Dead People." This large religious metropolis

Inside Temple at Kaminaljuyu

influenced the growth of villages and lesser ceremonial centers.

Government leadership was assumed by the people of Teotihuacan origin, who ruled efficiently until A.D. 500. The people of Kaminaljuyu traded with their neighboring cities and villages, and their influence and culture spread to other areas.

The people of Kaminaljuyu were skilled craftsmen who displayed their talents in ceramics, jade, wood carvings, stone mosaics, and pottery. Gifted writers, they compiled almanacs and codices and decorated them with pictures of their religious lore.

The religion was dedicated to a number of gods: rain gods and little squat gods, but no Quetzatcoatl. Human sacrifice appears to have been practiced by removal of the heart from the living.

Codz-Pop, The Palace of the Masks, Kabah

kabah

Corbelled arch at Kabah which stands at the end of an ancient Mayan road

Kabah is a large ancient site located south of Uxmal in the Yucatan Peninsula of Mexico. The buildings rise on a series of artificial platforms; one of the most outstanding is the Codz-Pop, whose facade is completely decorated with masks of the ancient rain god Chac. There were originally 270 masks, and they are often referred to as the mask of the hook-nosed rain god.

The builders made extensive use of columns with capitals, or motifs, decorated lintels, and groups of columns. An archway west of the main complex of buildings is the beginning of a highway leading to Uxmal.

Although the Codz-Pop is now mostly in ruins, enough remains to give us an idea of what it was like. In contrast to the Governor's Palace at Uxmal, the Codz-Pop has rooms on different levels and possibly was designed to have two stories, with one set back behind the other. But the second story was never built; instead, an enormous roof comb was erected upon the nucleus that had been prepared. It is possible that after the facade was finished the builders were disappointed and decided to complete the structure in a simpler fashion than had originally been planned.

The decoration on the facade of the Codz-Pop is, in fact, overpowering. Rows of enormous masks cover every square foot of surface, and not only the front but also the sides and perhaps the wall behind were covered with showy but overcrowded decorations. Such elaboration does not seem to conform with the sober and refined spirit of the Classic Maya. Perhaps this resulted from the particular social and political make-up of these cities, where frequently the palaces and residences—that is, dwellings for man—were more important than temples dedicated to gods.

La Venta

Olmec monument at the Parque de La Venta

The Olmec culture of La Venta in southern Mexico is dated somewhere near 880 B.C. Before settling on this site, the Olmecs were thought to have lived in San Lorenzo. Their community commenced around 1160 B.C., making it one of the oldest known in Mexico or Central America.

Large, freestanding basalt sculptures of heads were made by the Olmecs and are believed to be portraits of Olmec lords. These stone monuments cannot be directly dated by radiocarbon method, but associated artifacts can. The Olmecs must have been unusually gifted in engineering as well as in art, since the material from which these great carvings were made had to be hauled from the Tuxla Mountains, far to the northwest of La Venta.

The massive heads, some measuring almost ten feet in height, are one of the triumphs of ancient American art, yet their function and purpose remain a mystery. Several rectangular stones, which we sometimes call altars, are also found in this area, and although styles changed, the practice of building altars continued through all stages of Mesoamerican art. The altars at La Venta are trimmed in a twisted rope design, the same design used by the Phoenicians. Other features include bearded faces and upturned toes.

La Venta eventually became a great religious ceremonial center, drawing people from far and near to worship Quetzalcoatl. It is believed by some that infant sacrifice was practiced here, along with burnt offerings. The cross was carved into the stone walls five centuries before the birth of Christ.

The people used asphalt paving into which serpentine chips were set to form mosaics. Also found with the serpentine chips were little talismans of jade (an opalescent bluish or emerald green stone that was more highly prized than silver or gold).

Olmec figure

La Venta Olmec head

The triumphal arch of Labna

Labna

The Temple of Statues, Labna

Another city in the Puuc style is Labna, near Uxmal. Its most important building, although in a bad state of preservation, is the great palace. A long highway paved with stones leads from the palace toward the group of which the Mirador forms part. The front part of this temple is divided into three rooms—a central one flanked by two others. Behind the room in the middle is a sanctuary, roofed with the Mayan vault. Although much simpler than the facades of Palenque, this one features standing figures somewhat larger than natural size with big ornamental motifs in the middle. All the statues were placed on pedestals, but very little remains of these today.

A notable feature is the enormous roof comb more than four meters in height, which gives the temple a lofty and imposing appearance. Unlike the combs at Palenque, the one here is not placed on the transverse axis of the building; it is aligned with the facade, so that from the front of the building it looks like a prolongation of the latter, and it consists of only a single wall. This type of roof comb, while it corresponds to the Classic period, is characteristic of the Yucatan zone and not the zone of the great rivers, as is the case of those in Palenque.

In Yucatan, the ever-more-frequent use of the Mayan vault led to the erection of enormous vaulted doorways, such as those of the Governor's Palace at Uxmal. In Kabah this is carried even further, for at this site there is an independent Mayan gateway that puts one in mind of the triumphal arch. This photograph shows an arch of like monumental proportions at Labna, but it is not quite independent, since it serves as a doorway between two ceremonial patios. This huge ornamental gateway has a small roof comb above the main opening, as if it were a temple. The chambers on either side are in classic Puuc style: the lower part of the facade is entirely plain, while the upper part is decorated with the characteristic lattice pattern, with models of huts in the middle that perhaps formerly contained sculpture.

Mosaic wall pattern at Mitla

mitla

The Hall of Pillars, Mitla

About twenty-five miles southeast of Monte Alban, in the eastern valley of Oaxaca, lies a small set of buildings known as the ruins of Mitla. It is thought that the Zapotec culture of Monte Alban retreated to this area and settled here. In the Zapotec language Mitla is called "Yoo-paa" or "Place of the Dead."

Mitla is unique in that instead of large temple pyramids, there are several sprawling lower buildings, with flat roofs and courtyards. There are five separate complexes, with the court and the colonnade as the most prominent.

The most intriguing architectural achievements were the angular mosaics of protruding stones set in rhythmic repetition of geometric designs. It has been estimated that 130,000 individually cut stones were made to produce these beautiful mosaic patterns. No mortar was used between the pores, and the joints are barely visible, with the patterns blending flawlessly. One observer has referred to these mosaics as "petrified weaving." Some interior walls contrasted this design by displaying beautifully painted frescoes.

The people at Mitla believed in an afterlife, and great care was taken in tomb construction, such as the one found beneath the level of the pyramid floor in the form of a large cross. Sometimes the tomb contained only one body, but more often it was a collective grave.

Mitla represented a mixture of Zapotec and Mixteca-Puebla cultures. The people inherited much from their ancestors. However, they did innovate that which had come down to them and developed hieroglyphic writing, astronomy, mathematics, a calendrical system, and many realistic art pieces in paintings, bas-reliefs, architecture, corbeled vaulting, and tower roofing on temples. They created beautiful turquoise mosaics, miniature painted codices, and fine gold work.

Main Plaza at dawn, Monte Alban

monte alban

It would be hard to find a more beautiful site for a temple or religious center than the one atop a 1300-foot hill overlooking the beautiful and modern city of Oaxaca, Mexico. Oaxaca is 200 miles south and east of Mexico City. The ancient city of Monte Alban, built on just such a site approximately 800 years before Christ, still stands today; though a mere whisper of its ancient glory, it is still one of the most fabulous in all of Mexico. The site is 6500 feet above sea level. Cold is unknown in this area, and during the summer the heat is not excessive.

The ancient citizens of this era were not without their brilliant engineers, for the top of the entire hill was scraped off and leveled, in preparation for a magnificent complex of religious temples and buildings. Some of the structures were built over others. One of the most imposing houses of worship is the massive temple to the north of the quadrangle, which contains crumbling circular pillars and wide, majestic steps leading to the summit and covered with white stucco. This stairway represents three separate periods of construction and is believed to be the widest temple entrance in all America.

One of the buildings to the west of

Stelae at Monte Alban

the quadrangle contained a tomb of a very important personage, with its contents on display at the Museum of Anthropology in Mexico City. Another edifice to the south and west has been given the name Temple do los Danzantes, or Temple of the Dancers. Numerous bas-relief figures, carved on large stone slabs, and thought to resemble dancers, have been found in this building. Most recently, speculation has suggested certain anatomical sections of this carving. It is thought that perhaps this could be part of a medical school. Since the buildings in this complex seem to be spread about on the eminences of this mountain range, it does not appear that there was a dense population in the surrounding area. However, aerial photographs do indicate residences clustered in

The main plaza, Monte Alba

The main Temple at Monte Alban

the lower terraces of the mountainside. Cultures that include Olmec, Maya, Zapotec, Mixtec, and Aztec represent two thousand years of continuous occupation, which makes this archaeological site one of the longest continuously inhabited cities in Central America, anciently.

Monte Alban means, literally, "sacred mountain," and there are evidences here of an observatory, ball court, staircases, pyramids, temples, and burial vaults. Because of its topographic location, it also appears to have been an excellent site for a military center; however, no weapons or military evidences have been uncovered as yet.

Many exquisite artifacts have been unearthed in this ancient city. Alfonso Caso first began to excavate it in 1930. Beautiful gold work in the style of the Mixtec culture, articles of precious jade, obsidian, decorator shells, bracelets of gold and silver, a gold diadem, and an exquisite translucent vessel fashioned of onyx have been discovered here.

Other interesting aspects of these archaeological studies are the numerous examples of writing and numerals found. Some are on walls and others on stelae, accompanied with carvings of human figures. Some date glyphs have been deciphered but most of the hieroglyphs cannot be discerned. It is thought by some that writing in the New World began at Monte Alban.

It is still a mystery to students and scholars as to where this antiquated civilization obtained its water, and there are still a great many questions to be resolved concerning the inhabitants. But because of the treasures and wealth found in the tombs, Monte Alban is considered one of the richest archaeological finds in all America.

Even at present, market day in Oaxaca is notable. Great numbers of Zapotec and Mixtec Indians of the region come into town to sell their handmade products, such as pottery, shawls, and baskets. Many objects are of a beauty unequalled elsewhere in Mexico.

A stone stela at Monte Alban

The Palace of Palenque

palenque

The ruins of Palenque lie in the shadow of a lush mountainside east of Villahermosa, Mexico. The name comes from the Spanish and means palisade or place of war. A modern road takes you to the very center of this complex of ornate buildings, where one can still see evidence of recent diggings. Hills surrounding the ancient buildings reveal their man-made characteristics, and one suspects that the entire story has not yet been told.

Inside the Temple of Inscriptions, below ground level, is a burial tomb containing the body of an ancient and honored leader. On the surface of this tomb is engraven the Tree of Life insignia in the shape of a cross.

Sculptured figures and hieroglyphs cover many surfaces of the inner and outer walls of these buildings and courtyards. Scholars have dated these buildings back to before the time of Christ, and some researchers also believe this could be the cradle of the Mayan civilization.

Three tablets that were originally located in the Temple of the Cross, then were broken and moved several places, have now been gathered together and are on display in the Museum of Anthropology in Mexico City. The complete panel contains long rows of hieroglyphs on both sides and two standing figures facing the central carving of a tree in the form of a cross, thus giving the temple its name.

As one gazes over the countryside from atop the Temple of the Cross or the Temple of the Sun, he can see the vast plains of Tabasco and, on clear days, the Gulf of Mexico.

The Ostolum River flows through the center of the ruins of Palenque and was a source of water supply for the community. An artificial bed in the river suggests that it might have been used for bathing, swimming, or even religious rites.

The ball court was used both for playing ball and for important religious rites.

The Palace of Palenque

The different sides playing represented adverse deities. The priest could interpret the winning or losing of sides as prophecies whether the world would have droughts, famine, or good fortune.

The palace is a complex of buildings that rest upon a platform 300 feet long, 240 feet wide, and 3 feet high. The buildings are traced with patios, galleries, and stairways. A four-story tower rises from the complex, and a series of stairs starts at the first floor and extends to the top. It is believed this was used as both an astronomical observatory and a watchtower.

A reflection of a magnificent culture, Palenque stands as a mysterious and exquisite monument to the ancient and very civilized inhabitants of America.

Temples at Palenque

Cholula

Near the city of Puebla is a large man-made mountain, where we find the pyramid of Cholula, considered to be the largest in the world. The early Spanish destroyed most of the ancient structure and used the materials to build the town of Puebla. After serious excavation was begun, archaeologists found near the base of this tremendous structure many evidences of the building style used by the master builders who constructed it. It is thought by some scholars that there were several successive superpositions of buildings and that the innermost structure was erected as early as 2000 B.C.

The pyramid is 187 feet high, with its base covering approximately 44 acres. Although not as tall as the pyramid of Cheops, King of Egypt, it is almost twice as long as Cheops, and therefore probably had a larger mass. It took many thousands of workmen to build this magnificent structure, which the people called "Tlachi-hual-tepetl," meaning "man-made mountain."

The Catholic Church has constructed a building over the exact spot atop the pyramid where there was a building for worship purposes. Cholula is noted for its intricate system of passages. In one of these tunnels a burial section, apart from the main structure, was discovered.

Unexcavated pyramid of Cholula

To the west of this great pyramid is the beautiful extinct volcano, Popocatepetl. The plain of Cholula is somewhat barren, with lava covering part of the area. Although much of the original material is found in the homes of the surrounding area of Puebla, present archaeological work reveals a fascinating picture of the largest pyramid in the world.

Stone face worship, San Francisco

san francisco

Scattered throughout the country and jungle areas of southern Guatemala are places of worship without benefit of buildings or churches of any type. Large carved stone heads are the center of this outdoor worship, and the native Indians gather in groups or worship singly.

The service consists primarily in placing candles in front of the stone head, and incense, in the form of cedar chips placed in cans, is dangled on the end of two or three pieces of string. After lighting the incense, the person then swings it back and forth while he moves around the stone head, praying quietly. This procedure can last from several minutes to over an hour. While the father is doing this, any sons who accompany him stand by with folded hands and assist him when he beckons. Members of the family of the patriarch usually stay at home and maintain reverent silence until he returns.

The Indians say that although they are Christians and believe in Jesus Christ, they pay homage to these stone images to honor great spiritual leaders who lived prior to the time of Christ.

The Stone face of Baul

The Great Palace of Sayil

sayil

The construction and habitation of Sayil, the second of the three Puuc palaces included in this book, began sometime around A.D. 800. Many mounds are apparent but three buildings remain to testify of the people—the Mirador, the ball court, and the palace. In a bad state of preservation, the Sayil palace still reveals the great skill of the workmen.

The palace has three stories in stepped formation, the upper ones being supported by a solid fill set back from the floor below. They are connected in front by a great stairway of three flights, allowing access to terraces on each level. The lower facade, rather plain, has adornments of stucco or rows of little columns above the level of the doors. The middle story, by far the most elaborate, has a series of little columns on the mouldings, between the doors, and on the frieze. At the corners the characteristic masks may be seen, while in the middle of each section a carved panel shows a god descending—a frequent figure in Mesoamerica—flanked by two serpents in outline. The third story above each of the seven doors (five at the front and one on each side) has a human figure in stucco placed on a pedestal.

The whole structure is characterized by the desire for rich ornamentation contrasted with extensive plain surfaces. Not without justification do various scholars consider the Palace of Sayil to be one of the great triumphs of Mayan art.

We do not know who built or inhabited this vast seventy-room structure. The city, like Labna and Kabah, seems to have been abandoned before the arrival of Toltec influence in the tenth century A.D. There were no dated inscriptions here (or at least none have been found), but in neighboring Puuc cities, all the latest dates are around the middle of the ninth century except that of Uxmal, which gives the year 909.

Niche Pyramid, El Tajin

el tajin

El Tajin is on the gulf coast of Mexico, in the Veracruz area. It is 30 kilometers from the Gulf of Mexico and is only slightly above sea level, in a hot and humid climate. A compact group of temples, buildings, and palaces indicates influence from the Teotihuacan, Mayan, and Oaxaca cultures. However, some innovations make this ruin singularly attractive. The ornamental sculptured design of interlocking scrolls, along with other decorative designs, represents some of the finest sculpture in pre-Columbian America.

While the majority of the buildings still await excavation, the principal building, the Temple of the Niches, is one of the best known in Mexico. The temple, about 36 meters wide on each side and 25 meters high, is constructed in a ziggurat fashion. Each story has an extended panel and a projecting cornice, with panels decorated with niches or indentations. The latest research concludes that these niches, which were painted red with blue frames, were always empty and for decorative purposes only. There are even niches underneath the stairway at the front of the pyramid, indicating that the stairway was superimposed on the building. It is interesting to note that the number of niches totals 365, which seems to correlate in some way with the number of days in the year.

A tall pole was used in a ceremonial game called "voladores" (flying dancers). Five men participated; one stayed at the top of the pole while the others attached themselves to ropes, unwinding themselves from the top and assuming a bird-like flight in their descent.

There are several ball courts at Tajin, with sculptured figures on the walls depicting various ceremonies attached to the playing of this ancient religious game. Friezes and panels on the walls depict ritual scenes.

Found on the site are other buildings, called Lesser Tajins, decorated with friezes, panels, and facades. Stone carvings are also numerous. Another interesting and most unusual building is the Building of the Columns, which is adorned with Greek crosses.

tenayuca

The great Temple of Tenayuca, on the outskirts of Mexico City, is among the few known buildings dating from the period subsequent to the fall of Tula but prior to the triumph of Tenochtitlan. In this period (1200-1400), deceptively called Chichimec, its builders certainly copied the old architecture inherited from Tula, as the Aztecs were to do later. A characteristic feature is the Coatepantli, or wall of serpents; here, however, instead of running all around the pyramid, this chain of rather realistic reptiles encompasses three sides only. And it does not really form a wall sitting off an area devoted to occult ceremonies, as at Tula.

The principal innovation at Tenayuca makes for economy; instead of the pyramid's serving as a base to support a single temple, as had previously been the rule, it now holds two, each with its own stairway and low balustrade. This idea was to be used again in the great temple of Tenochtitlan, where the Aztecs placed over a single gigantic base both a temple to the God of War and a temple to the God of Rain.

We cannot judge the nature of the city or town that surrounded Tenayuca, since the area is now entirely built up, making archaeological exploration difficult. The temple itself was in ruins, making the work of reconstruction considerable. Like most temples in Mesoamerica, though, this edifice was originally covered with stucco and painted in vivid colors.

Plaza of Three Cultures known as Tlatilolco

tenochtitlan

Tenochtitlan (now the present site of Mexico City) was founded by the Aztec people about A.D. 1300 on the west shore of Lake Texcoco. After 150 years of war, the original site of Tenochtitlan became the ancient capital of the powerful Aztec nation.

In 1519, when Hernando Cortez arrived in Tenochtitlan, he found a rich, flourishing culture. The Spaniards strode along wide streets with high mansions built of a red, porous stone, nearly all having roof gardens full of luxuriant plants. The common people lived in huts built of mud and rushes.

Cortez found Tenochtitlan to be a maze of architectural wonder, with pyramids, pillars, arcades, buildings with many halls, towers, temples, barbers' salons, apothecaries, and the Palace of Axayacatl.

These early visitors wrote that Tenochtitlan had 60,000 houses, 300,000 inhabitants, streets swept and washed clean, many fountains and fish ponds, schools, and large markets where people could buy and sell a fantastic array of goods.

In some parts of the city canals took the place of streets. From the Plaza of Three Cultures (known also as Tlatilolco), one can view a scene unique and historical in nature. In the foreground is the restored portion of the city of Tenochtitlan; behind this is an old colonial Spanish cathedral, with rows of modern apartment houses behind it.

Tenochtitlan had a complex social and political government. According to its geography, the city was divided into 20 calpullis (clans), with each calpullis governed by the group of families in its borders.

Each section had its own schools, priests, and temples. Children were taught farming, arts and crafts, warfare, history, citizenship, and religious practices. Boys who wanted to enter the priesthood and girls who wanted to become priestesses were trained in special schools. Priests were in charge of all education.

Looking down avenue of the Dead from the top of the Temple of the Moon

teotihuacan

A vast complex of ruins is found at Teotihuacan, about 30 miles northeast of present-day Mexico City. It was called "the place where the gods reside" by the Aztecs who arrived on the scene years after the city was in its prime. This ancient city covers about eight square miles and boasted a population of over 100,000. Various dates have been ascribed to the city, but it appears that the culture commenced in 300 B.C. and reached a decline in A.D. 1000. It is deservedly one of the most popular tourist attractions in Mexico.

The largest building is the Pyramid of the Sun, which rises 210 feet high from a square base more than 738 feet long on each side. Covering an area of 544,644 square feet, with a volume of 3.25 million cubic feet, it is larger in volume than the pyramid of Cheops in Egypt and contains about a million tons of sun-dried mud bricks. No second structure has been built over the first, as with many pyramids. The second most prominent building is the Temple of the Moon. The heart of the city was this ancient ceremonial center.

Concourses, plazas, smaller temples, palaces, public buildings, and many residential units are found throughout the area. Some walls are plastered and others contain murals. Cement streets cover

Temple of Quetzalcoatl, at Teotihuacan.

Temple of the Moon, Teotihuacan

underground drain conduits. Craftsmen, painters, sculptors, masons, and artisans contributed their wares and talents to make Teotihuacan truly beautiful.

In front of the Temple of the Moon are several symmetrical buildings, similar in height and size and arranged to give the scene magnificent splendor. Teotihuacan appears to have been the focus and coordinating religious center, and its influence pervaded the entire Valley of Mexico.

Quetzalcoatl was their central figure of deity. This god brought good ways of life and fought with the gods of evil. Sacrifices were practiced on now-worn altars. A temple dedicated to Quetzalcoatl has been partially restored. On either side of the staircase are large serpent heads backed by a circular row of feathers. The serpent motif, exquisitely formed, appears repeatedly on this temple. One wonders what tools were used to create such detailed and exquisite carvings.

Along the "Avenue of the Dead" is the Temple of Agriculture. In it are many murals that depict the people engaged in various types of agricultural pursuits. The people also used a calendar system.

The government was highly organized into a theocracy, under priest rule. This theocracy seems to have held the city people together, helping maintain their highly civilized way of life for 600 years.

Temple of the Moon, Teotihuacan

Altar 5, Tikal

Temple II as seen from the top of Temple I

Stone stela 16 at Tikal

tikal

Tikal is a pre-Columbian ruin located in the country of Guatemala. Close to the border of British Honduras, this important archaeological site is in the tropical jungle of Central America. One can reach it by flying from Guatemala City and landing on an airstrip near the center of the Tikal ruin complex. The University of Pennsylvania has been developing this area for a number of years.

By current dating methods, these ruins date from approximately 600 B.C., which makes some of the structures 2500 years old.

A visitor at Tikal finds this tropical area humid, warm, and, depending upon the time of year, usually rainy. He can sometimes see monkeys swinging through the trees. Many colorful and graceful varieties of birds exist here, including the parrot and heron. Beyond the ruins live the jaguar, puma, and ocelot, as well as small deer and some snakes. The jungle is made up of zapote, logwood, mahogany, Spanish cedars, ceibas, sapodilla, and many low and high palms. All of these are interspersed with dense jungle vegetation.

The ruins are at the center of a 222-square-mile national park, where a museum houses many of the artifacts found there.

An official expedition was made into Tikal in 1848, although it has been suspected that Spanish missionaries previously ventured into this same general area. Modern studies of Tikal commenced with the work of Sylvanus G. Morley, his main concern being Mayan writing.

There are over 3,000 separate structures in Tikal, including temples, palaces, shrines, sacrificial altars, ceremonial platforms, residences, ball courts, terraces, causeways, bathing places, and more than 200 stone monuments. Over 100,000 tools, ceremonial objects, personal ornaments, and other items have been unearthed. Absent are the uses of gold and other metals, but beautiful jade jewelry and stone tools have been unearthed. There are also no underground rivers or wells such as the cenotes in Yucatan. More than a million potsherds have been collected in this area. Almost without exception it was found that the existing structures have been built over previous construction. Sometimes there is evidence that there were more than one or two underlying structures.

The age of the buildings at Tikal is a fascinating study. Some scholars conclude that a pre-Classic period began at Tikal circa 600 B.C., a Classic period at

A.D. 250, and a late Classic period at A.D. 550. This last period would include the collapse of Tikal about A.D. 900. Most of what is seen at Tikal in the massive structures is portions of the late Classic period, about A.D. 700.

Tikal is built around the Great Plaza. The most magnificent structure still standing in this grand acropolis has been designated as Temple I, or Temple of the Giant Jaguar. This limestone building, 145 feet above the Great Plaza and built about A.D. 700, has nine sloping terraces and three rooms set behind each other in tandem fashion. It appears that the temple was painted in cream, red, and other colors, perhaps green and blue.

The temple chambers were spanned by high corbeled vaults, and Tikal is famous for its superb, fantastically carved wooden lintels. Inside, the towering Temple I consists of solid construction and is thought to be younger than Temple II.

Both temples appear to have been used for religious ceremonies and astronomical pursuits of the priests. Near the ruins are large carved monoliths, called stelae, and sacrificial altars. The inscriptions on these stelae were not meant to be permanent, because many of the carved stones were purposely destroyed by the Classic Mayas, and they were careful to smash the faces of the individuals depicted.

It is now believed that permanent records were kept in folded books, and three such Mayan codices have survived.

In the northern part of the main plaza are the remains of as many as 100 buildings, with some buried over several earlier structures, one atop the other, and the earliest dating back to 600 B.C.

North Acropolis, Tikal

Temple I, Tikal

Temple of Tzintzuntzan

tzintzuntzan

The ruins of Tzintzuntzan are located on the shores of Lake Patzcuaro in the State of Michoacan in Mexico. The reconstructed buildings combined the less-used circular terraced construction with the rectangular buildings that were more popular anciently.

The pottery from this ruin has been dated at approximately A.D. 500-700. According to scholars, the sculptures bear traces of the Teotihuacan style, developed during the post-Classic period and identified with the Tarascan culture. The Tarascans were able to withstand the aggressions of the Aztec Empire and therefore were considered powerful. They expanded from this area and took possession of most of the State of Michoacan, plus Jalisco and Colima. The Tarascans, superb metallurgists, were among the first people in the Mexico region to develop and employ the techniques of casting, gilding, soldering, alloying, and smelting, using gold and silver.

Tzintzuntzan is a small but lovely ruin upon a hill overlooking the city of San Pablo. The largest building is terraced and is about 1400 feet by 900 feet wide. One can climb to the top of the terrace by means of a flight of steps 325 feet wide. A chieftain's tomb at the foot of the stairs

Wall section of the Temple at Tzintzuntzan

contained ornaments, copper and gilt half-moons, funeral offerings, bells, filigree work; and masterpieces in obsidian and hard stone. People who had been sacrificed to the gods were buried around the king.

Pillars and the five-stepped main pyramid of Tula

A good example of the corbeled arch is found in the group of buildings known as the Nunnery. The tallest building is the Temple of the Magician, whose sides are rounded with three terraced areas and a worship building on top. The Pyramid of the Magician is shaped somewhat elliptically at the base, with other temples on the top.

Masks of the rain god mounted one above another ornament the front of the Nunnery. Stones cut precisely from an extraordinarily beautiful mosaic pattern become the upper part of the wall facing the Nunnery's four-sided patio. Slender columns are part of the decor on the lower part of the wall, while grillework mosaics form the design on the upper wall. The Nunnery has a cloister effect, with its numerous individual rooms. Only a base now remains of a statue of a large jaguar that stood in the center of the court, which measures 215 by 150 feet. A number of masks of the rain god and of the god Chac decorated the outsides of this building.

The archaeological city of Uxmal, thrice built, is considered one of the most successful architectural achievements of the Mayan civilization. The inhabitants made use of cisterns to catch rain water for drinking and extensive culinary purposes. This region does not have water holes, so rain water was looked upon with great reverence.

A small ball court still remains at Uxmal. It had several long row-like buildings that were probably used as grandstands.

North end of Nunnery

Masks of the rain-god at the temple of Xlapak

xlapak

If you are traveling through the jungles of the Yucatan Peninsula, from the ruins of Kabah to Labna, portions of other ruins are visible. Xlapak is one of the ancient Puuc cities only partially excavated, but a beautiful corner of the palace, with its three superimposed masks of the god of rain, can be seen. Short columns separate the decorated area above from the plain area below. In the center the masks assume a geometric form, while to their left can be seen the beginning of a "xicolcoli-uhqui," the fret that in a multitude of variations represents a stylized serpent and was used in all Mesoamerica from the end of the pre-Classic period.

This photograph evokes the romantic atmosphere of drawings from the middle of the nineteenth century in which wild plants are shown growing in profusion over stones carved with so much effort and application in ancient times, slowly destroying the masonry until finally it falls to the ground.

John Lloyd Stephens, well named the Herodotus of Mayan archaeology, illustrates his second book, *Incidents of Travel in Yucatan*, which appeared in 1843, with numerous drawings made by that enterprising London architect Frederick Catherwood, who accompanied him on his trips. Current tastes, the solitude of the ruins, and his profound interest in the ancient Maya and their works led Catherwood to populate his accurate drawings with trees and plants, which, far from weakening their archaeological value, renders them more realistic.

Much mystery surrounds these unexcavated ruins, and the beautiful vegetation and foliage covering the buildings make the scene even more intriguing.

Central plaza at Zaculeu

Zaculeu

Zaculeu, which means "white earth," is located on a plateau in the Guatemalan Highlands, close to the city of Huehuetenango in the shadow of the Cuchumatanes Mountains. Once an important ceremonial center, it was built sometime in the early post-Classic period. Some Mayas were still living there at the time of the Spanish Conquest.

A number of ancient buildings were restored at Zaculeu by the United Fruit Company and the Guatemalan government's Institute of Anthropology and History between February 1946 and April 1949. The job of restoration at Zaculeu represents one of the most complete of any ancient ruin in Guatemala.

The city, which is dominated by a large, impressive temple, a ball court, and smaller buildings and temples, is completely surrounded by rivers, streams, trenches, and moats—its main type of defense.

Zaculeu's ceremonial importance is characterized by forty-three structures arranged in courts, or plazas. The largest temple was built in terrace fashion, with rough masonry walls covered with plaster, and several sets of stairs leading to the top of the temple.

Many buildings in the city have three

Temple altar at Zaculeu

doorways and three rooms, which some believe may represent the members of the deity.

The main portions of the buildings surrounding the ball court are raised platforms with stairs for spectators to easily reach their seats.

When excavated, the area revealed the foundations of long-removed altars, with plain architecture and none of the ornate trimmings of Tikal. Zaculeu also was a burial ground; the graves housed not only the dead but such artifacts as beads, jade jewelry, bowls, jars, effigy pendants, figurines of all sizes and shapes, and pottery.

Facade of the main Temple-pyramid at Xochicalco

Temple at Xochicalco

xochicalco

Xochicalco was one of the first sites to which Mexican archaeologists of the eighteenth century devoted their attention. Alexander von Humboldt, who never visited Xochicalco, availed himself of these pioneer works in order to write a far from accurate description of the site. We now know not only a great deal more about the building described by Humboldt and other scholars of this day, but of various additional ones that have since been explored and in which a great number of objects were found.

The pyramid that was initially uncovered is still outstanding among the monuments at Xochicalco. It is not for its size that it is remarkable—since it is relatively small—but for the low reliefs that originally covered the entire structure. The reliefs on the lower section, comprising a tall sloping base and a wide cornice corresponding to the panel in Teotihuacan-style architecture, show an abundance of motifs. The detail to be seen in this plate represents a plumed serpent—the god Quetzalcoatl—with a skillfully carved head from which a forked tongue protrudes, an undulating body, and a tail terminating in feathers. As with all great ceremonial serpents of Mesoamerica, the serpent is depicted with an eyebrow, as well as a beard under the lower jaw.

One of the spaces formed by the reptile's curves contains hieroglyphs with the sign for fire. The other is even more important, for it shows a seated figure holding one hand over the breast and wearing an enormous headdress of plumes. The posture, the design, and the general aspect of this individual recall—even if it is only remotely—a Mayan priest.

On the uppermost level of the ancient city of Xochicalco, built on a moderately high hill, are the remains of a fortress. This would indicate that the site could be defended, unlike Teotihuacan, which is situated in a broad plain. The city of Xochicalco is thought to have been built about the eighth and ninth centuries A.D.

On a flat area and on a lower level than the monument of Quetzalcoatl is situated the enormous ball court. It is 69 meters long, being therefore much larger than the one at Monte Alban but almost identical to the one at Tula, not only in size but in general design. Both are laid out in the customary fashion, the field being in the shape of a capital I flanked on each side by a sloping embankment ending in a wall; in the center of each of the two walls is a large stone ring, one of which can be clearly seen in this view. It is assumed that the ball was meant to pass through these rings, an event that must have been rare indeed if we take into consideration the manner of playing, the size of the ball, and the relatively small orifice. The platforms behind the walls, where the remains of small buildings can still be seen, are not identical: on the north side the natural rock has been utilized; to the south the platform begins on a lower level and follows the slant of the hill. Slopes, porticos, and staircases compensate for this difference.

In distance can be seen remains of a building known as La Malinche, joined to the ball court by a broad avenue 50 meters long.

The fortress city of Yagul

yagul

In the valley of Oaxaca, on a raised platform area, lies the restored ruin of Yagul. There are various levels on this hillside site, and the largest building (Palace of Six Patios) is a huge structure with more than thirty rooms, most of which are ranged around these patios.

The whole unit has only one entrance, which leads into a long hallway that divides it into two unequal parts. In the western section are four patios; in the eastern section are two, which are better constructed and more elaborate. As at Mitla, portions of the exterior walls here were covered by stone mosaics, but these have disappeared and explorations have recovered but few of the remains, possibly because stone from this ancient city was used to build part of the modern town of Tlacolula, its neighbor. Many of the walls still have the original red plaster covering them.

On a lower level is another large unit comprising the Sala del Consejo (Assembly Hall), a vast room similar to that at the entrance to the main palace at Mitla but without the monolithic columns; other civic buildings, the ball court, and other patios surrounded by large rooms. Only a tall pyramid, now in very bad condition, suggests that a temple once stood here. Much higher up from where this photograph was taken is the fortress, formed in part by natural rocks and in part by stone walls.

This ruin did not emphasize the religious motif; rather, there are indications that it was a military or administrative unit. From any part of this ruin, one has a panoramic view of the beautiful valley of Oaxaca, and this may have been the reason why Yagul was built in the hills—as a fortress and protection for the cities below.

south america

PERU

Peru gets its name from a river in southern Colombia. The name stuck with the Spanish sailors and conquistadores and replaced the Indian name of Tahuantinsuyu, which by interpretation means four quarters. The Indian population of Peru today is probably six to seven million and makes up the largest and most compact indigenous group in the Americas.

The Spanish conquest of Peru destroyed the social and economic structure of the Inca empire, and the distribution of the population was changed. The people were forced to regroup into villages where they could be supervised. Titles to property were abolished; their deities were forgotten. The lowest class seemed to float about, becoming servants or serfs.

The potato is the most precious gift Peru has given to the Old World. By patience, trial, and error the Indians changed the small-sized wild tuber into one of our favorite foods.

Peru is divided naturally into three areas: the low arid coast, the tropical humid eastern lowlands, and the cool highlands. The Humboldt current brings cold water from Chile along the coast of Peru, resulting in the eastbound winds dropping their moisture at sea and depositing no rain on the coast. There are years when no drop of rain falls in southern coastal Peru and northern Chile and, as a result, there is very little plant life there. Occasionally where a valley shows lush green fields, a life-giving river comes from the mountains.

Much of central Peru is uncultivable because the snow-clad mountains are too high for agriculture and people. The valleys, however, are fertile and populated with many natives. The Cuzco basin, with an average elevation of 11,200 feet, was the seat of the Inca empire.

The Indians of Peru represent about 40 percent of the population. The modern Indian, who is a descendant of the Inca, has a stature that is rather short, but his body build is massive. The Quechua Indian is beardless, and his chest, shoulders, and hips are well developed. The height of the men averages five feet two and one-half inches, and the women, four feet nine and one-half inches. The broadness of their upper torso is probably related to the unusual size of their lungs, caused by lack of oxygen in the high altitude.

As the ancient Peruvians developed, agriculture replaced fishing, hunting, and wild-food gathering. Although the people still fished and hunted, corn became their staple food. With it came peanuts, squashes, avocados, yucca, and manioc.

Llamas and dogs were an important part of native life. Irrigation was developed, terraces were built, and fertilization was practiced. The homes were apparently small one-room structures with thatched roofs.

Religion developed into an advanced formalized function and became a very important part of the Incan life. Temples were built and masonry work became an art, with intricate stone and cement work. Some adobe bricks were made where rock was not available.

The dead were revered and placed in arid places in relatively deep graves; these graves were found to include food and vocational tools, presumably of the deceased, and there is evidence of a belief in immortality. Pottery became an accomplished art, with the stirrup-spouted jar a common shape.

The Peruvian commoner's life was rather monotonous in comparison to our standards. The man tilled his fields and those of the church and state, possibly served a tour of duty in the army or mines, and made regular trips to the markets. The woman spent most of her time fixing meals and spinning and weaving. Religious ceremonies were probably the highlight of their lives.

Metallurgy made its appearance early; gold, silver, and copper were used primarily, and later tin was combined with copper to form bronze. Techniques include hammering, embossing, annealing, welding, soldering, strap joining, incising, champleve, cut-out designs, and the bi-metal object. Much of the gold was painted with colored pigments.

Master artisans developed in their use of semiprecious stones. Bone, shell, and wood were also raw materials for beads, pendants, rings, and combs. Such utilitarian objects as bowls, spatulas, needles, daggers, spoons, bags, baskets, stone and wood boxes, and warfare instruments were manufactured.

Aqueducts and canals were found in every valley, and some of these projects demonstrated exceptional engineering ability. Even water purification plants were established. Some of these canals are still in use today; the aqueduct at Ascope in the Chicama Valley is nearly a mile long and 50 feet high, and has a content of over a million cubic yards of earth.

Two- and three-story temples with heavy slab roofs and subterranean houses and galleries with as many as two stories underground were built in the northern highlands.

Peruvian culture reached its climax in the Classic era, approximately 300 B.C. to A.D. 500.

We must never forget that these ancestors of the Peruvian Indians created one of the most original civilizations the world has known, and made an area habitable that was barely so by nature.

Religion

Fasting, confession, prayers, animal sacrifice, and later human sacrifice were part of the religion of the early Peruvians. One observance was interesting: after penance for sinning, the sinner washed in a stream so that the sin might be borne away. They believed in a god called Wiracocha, or Viracocha, who was the world god. The characteristics of this South American god are strikingly similar to those of the Mesoamerican Quetzalcoatl. This god provided an answer for the people as to how the world began. Virococha had the form of a man, and it was thought by the natives that he created the sub-gods and goddesses—sun, moon, stars, etc. At his side was a second being, "the Transformer," who completed Viracocha's work and instructed the people in the rudiments of civilization.

After many adventures, Viracocha reached the coast, where he cast his mantle on the sea; the mantle became a raft, and in this he vanished over the horizon.

Medicine

R. L. Moodie states:

> I believe it to be correct to state that no primitive or ancient race of people anywhere in the world had developed such a field of surgical knowledge as had the pre-Columbian Peruvians. Their surgical attempts are truly amazing and include amputations, excisions, trephining, bandaging, bone transplants,

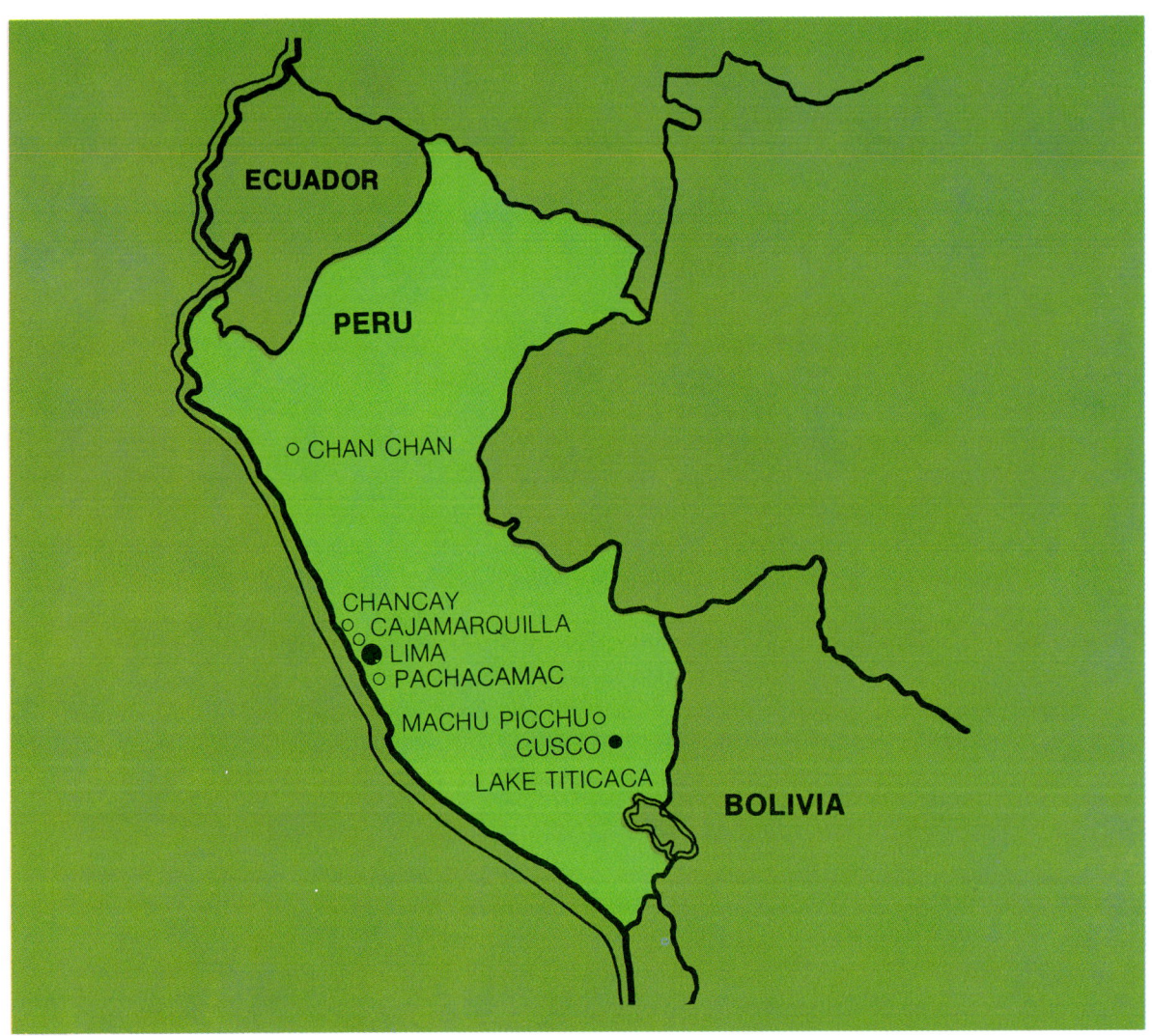

cauterizations and other less evident procedures. (Roy L. Moodie, *Studies in Paleopathology, XXI: Injuries to the Head Among the Pre-Columbian Peruvians,* Annals of Medical History, vol. 9 [1927], p. 278.)

Most of the information on Peruvian surgery is based on the skeletal remains and from the pottery rather than from the chroniclers. Probably coca was used as an anaesthetic. Forceps, the tourniquet, and bandaging with gauze and cotton were used. Trephining is thought to have been performed to relieve compressions, the result of fractures, to release demons, but also perhaps to repair cranial fractures from war. The incisions may have been round or rectangular and were performed by scraping, sawing, and cutting with obsidian, copper, or bronze instruments.

Calendar

The Peruvians did not have as detailed a calendar system as did the Mayas, and probably for the commoner a lunar year was established by each new moon. The quipu, the instrument for record-keeping, consisted basically of a series of strings in which knots were tied. The great variation possible in the color and position of the strings, and the nature, number, and position of the knots, permitted its use for numerical records and mnemonic purposes.

Highways

There were two main north-south roads, one along the coast and one through the highlands. Transverse roads connected these, and minor roads connected each village. The north-south road started in Colombia and ended in Chile, and some have computed this to be approximately 3,000 miles long. These roads followed a straight line wherever possible and zigzagged up slopes. Many were paved and were from three feet wide to 100 feet wide. It has been estimated there were 9,500 miles of road in the South American system. In marshy places causeways were built over streams, and bridges and even tunnels have been found. Some suspension bridges were supported by ropes 16 inches in diameter. The irrigation program included causeways up to 50 feet high in low-lying land.

Arts and Crafts

It is in creating smaller objects that the Peruvian artist was most skillful, such objects as pottery, textiles, and metal work. The architecture was massive rather than beautiful.

The ancient Peruvians performed every method of textile weaving or decoration now known, and made finer products than are made today. The dyes used were mostly vegetable but other sources are known, and one researcher has distinguished 190 hues of color in the Paracas textiles.

The possible variations and forms of pottery manufacturing are so great that archaeologists can distinguish the ceramic product made in any region.

In metallurgy, gold was the first metal to be worked; it is thought that it was first beaten into thin plates and then tooled or hammered into designs. Silver and copper were used later, and tin was combined with copper to form bronze. Even platinum was used on the coast of Ecuador, and a few pieces of iron have been found in Peru.

Among the civilizations and cultures of South America, some of the most outstanding were the Inca, Chancay, Mochica, Chimu, Chavin, Nasca, Paracas. A short description of each of these cultures follows, and photographs and descriptions of some of the representative ruins are shown.

THE INCAS

The Incas were the principal ruling power during the Spanish invasion of South America. Some have estimated that their culture became distinct about A.D. 1000. Besides Peru, the Inca empire included much of Ecuador, Chile, and Bolivia, linked by mountain and coastal highways that included bridges and tunnels. The conquerors found an efficient administration and a system of communication through networks of highways and runners. The Incas were accomplished agriculturalists and developed a superior way of life. Since they were a conquering people, they were not outstanding in their architecture.

The Incas are thought to have numbered at least 16,000,000 people at one time.

The land was divided according to the needs of the family, and each married couple was assigned one-half acre; each boy child was allowed one-half acre, and each girl child one-fourth acre.

Among the weapons of the Inca group were slings, spear throwers, and boles—three stone balls joined by cords. Some groups also used the bow and arrow. The Inca soldier protected himself by means of square or round shields, helmets, and cloth tunics stuffed with cotton.

The tremendous irrigation work of the Incas has been described by Garcilaso de la Vega as "superior and marvelous" in comparison with any other in the world.

The Incas became proficient in working with gold and silver. They produced an assortment of necklaces, rings, nose jewels, earrings, brooches, and gold belts. Some household items were made of precious metals, such as drinking and eating utensils. Gold was one of the things for which the Incas were famous, but much of this gold was, unfortunately, destroyed when the Conquistadores forced them to melt their treasures into ingots for shipment back to Spain.

MOCHI OR MOCHICA CULTURE

This culture, which developed mostly during the late pre-Classic period (c. 300 B.C. - A.D. 500) of Peru, demonstrates the high level of excellence achieved by the cultures of this period. The Mochi lived on the northern coast of Peru; other great cultures, Nasca and Paracas, lived on the southern coast.

These people were primarily agricultural peoples, interested in nature and life as it actually happened. Hunting of animals was restricted to the upper-class as a sport; men hunting with blow guns and shooting birds are depicted on pottery jars. Fields and crops were watered by canals. The domesticated llama and guinea pig provided most of the meat diet, with the exception of abundant fish.

The Mochi erected enormous temples. Their Temple of the Sun is estimated to have 130 million adobe bricks. Their forts are often surrounded by walls, and roads of 33 feet in width were found to be standard.

The Mochica culture is noted mostly for its naturalistic ceramics. Their pottery is extremely impressive, in a variety of shapes and sizes. So expressive are the head jars that native inhabitants would take them as portraits; some were caricatures with modern poncho-like shirts. Two-piece pottery molds have been found, with stirrup spouts added. Geometrical painting of the jars in black and red paints was very popular. The painted pottery depicts humans who suffered from a variety of diseases, amputation of limbs, lips, or nose for punishment, and medicinemen working cures for the unfortunate. These items indicate that amputation, bone setting, and circumcision were practiced.

Mochicas were divided into classes. The wealthiest (upper class) dressed in the finest linens, feathers, and jewelry. The middle class dressed in simple cloth shirts with breech clouts. Most men wore ear or nose jewelry. The warrior class dressed in skirts, metal armor, and helmets. Prisoners, the lowest class, are depicted naked with ropes around their necks. Eventually they were sacrificed to the gods.

Casting, soldering, annealing, and gilding were all part of their metallurgy, and alloys of gold, silver and copper were used. The Mochica culture was influenced by secular and political events, but the common religion seemed to be the determining factor of their history.

The attributes of the Mochi people demonstrate one of the most dynamic and aggressive cultures of the Peruvian pre-Columbian civilizations.

CHAVIN CULTURE

The Chavin culture had its beginning about 900 B.C. or earlier in the northern coastal areas of Peru. Some think that the culture extended north into Equador, and some influence has been seen as far south as Chile and Argentina. The common factor in this culture was the manner in which art was subordinated to religion. The religion seemed to have motifs, including the jaguar, the serpent, the bird of prey, and an alligator form. Yale archaeologist Michael Coe thinks that art forms in Mexico are similar to those of the Chavin culture and suggests that there was a maritime trade network between the Pacific coast of Middle America and Ecuador and Peru.

Chavin de Huantar appears to be the largest of the cult centers and is located 140 miles north of Lima, Peru, in the small Mosna Valley 10,000 feet higher than Lima. Underground passageways, ramps, and stairways characterize this site. It does not appear that the majority of people lived at the site; their homes were probably on the outskirts of the city. The houses were probably one-room rectangular structures with thatched gable roofs. Religion was advanced, and the temples were well-planned and well-used, with numerous rooms, platforms, and steps. Agriculture was the main source of food supply.

Skull deformation was a common practice. Burials seem to present the idea that these people believed strongly in an afterlife. Food and drink as well as pottery and other items were interred with the body. There are indications of more than one burial of a body, since some of the bones have been covered with a red powder or pigment.

The potters of the Chavin culture were classed as excellent except for the technical development of that skill, which came later. They formed pottery of simple shapes but with thick rims and stirrup spouts.

Tapestry and embroidery were made, as well as a lace-like gauze, but not with all the later techniques found elsewhere. Cotton was apparently the material used.

Gold seems to be the predominant metal, although silver and copper were also used. Many techniques of metallurgy were employed, and this industry flourished.

CHANCAY

South of Chimu, a smaller state produced a culture known as the Chancay. The most remarkable urban center of this culture is Cajamarquilla. Adobe was the main building material. The most striking but crude pottery on the central coast of Peru was produced by these people. The artistry is not sophisticated, but the shapes and variety are interesting, including an egg-shaped jar with a flaring collar and a pair of small loop handles. Black or brown on white predominates in their pottery, which seems to recall the early Chimu art and at the same time that of Nasca.

This great culture is noted for its textiles, for the weavers of Chancay were magnificently skilled in their craft and the use of a great range of colors. Their embroideries and lace showed their technical mastery.

These people developed skilled techniques in gold-copper alloys. Clay panpipes are found in Chancay. It is here that the graves are covered with poles or rough stone vaults.

CHIMU

The Chimu, a northern coastal people of Peru, was a culture that developed between A.D. 1000 and 1300. The large fertile river valleys, which receive heavy rainfall, supported a great concentration of people. The capital of the Chimu was Chan Chan, near the present site of Trujillo.

The later Chimu culture was contemporary with the Inca but produced no outstanding ceramic art. They used molds and mass-produced their wares. Four-fifths of their pottery was black, and the stirrup pottery predominated. There are some double-spouted vessels that also seem to be whistles, for when liquid is poured out one spout, the air coming in the other spout causes the pot to whistle.

The Chimu, like the Mochicas, practiced extensive irrigation.

The ruins of Chan Chan cover over eight square miles. Some of the walls in and around the city are covered with arabesque decorations in low relief and probably were made by impressions of molds. The designs are of small repeated motifs in rows similar to textile designs. Many of the designs include animals. Some wall paintings have also been found.

When the Inca advanced on the Chimu, the struggle was short and uneven. The Chimu ruler wished to fight on to death, but his counselors induced him to surrender.

NASCA CULTURE

The Nasca culture of Peru was unknown until 1901, when it was discovered by Max Uhle. The beautiful polychrome pottery vessels for which the Nasca culture is most noted are found in major museums throughout the world. The Nasca Valley is located more than a hundred miles southeast of Paracas, and there are indications the Paracas culture preceded the Nasca culture and possibly gave birth to the latter. The Nasca culture seems to date from 200 B.C. to A.D. 600. An ancient highway connected Nasca with Cuzco.

The Nascas built no large structures of adobe, and there was no stone masonry of this period in this area. There were no large towns; the houses were clustered in small village-like groups.

Nasca textiles are beautiful but not as technically elaborate as those of the Paracas. Practically all of the Peruvian textile processes was known to the Nasca weaver. The range of colors used is amazing; 190 tints have been identified.

Metallurgy among the Nasca was far less than among the Mochi. Only gold seemed to be known, and it was not cast but was pounded into thin sheets, cut into various shapes, and decorated with designs.

The Nascas had an interesting custom that some have attributed to their religion. They made designs, including the outlines of some animals, on the level surface; these large designs can be seen only from an airplane. It is therefore supposed that they were made to please celestial deities. Some of these lines are thought to point toward solstitial or equinoctial points and therefore become astronomically important. Since they were not able to observe their work and thereby gain a perspective, they must have worked from models. They also developed a calendar system.

The City of Cajamarquilla, Peru

machu picchu

The renowned ruins of Machu Picchu were discovered and explored in July 1911 by Hiram A. Bingham. On the left bank of the River Urubamba, at 8,875 feet altitude and 70 miles northwest from Cuzco, the ruins comprise an area of approximately two square miles and occupy the entire top of a hill so steep that accessibility is difficult by any means.

This fortress was built entirely of white granite and has palaces, temples, towers, fountains, baths, and residential districts. The many terraces are connected by steps, and it has been estimated that there are 109 flights and approximately 3000 steps. The terraces have been and are still used to grow food products.

Machu Picchu is naturally defended by the precipices of the mountains and made even more formidable by walls and moats. Much of the masonry consists of rock walls of the Cuzco type, with bricks cut to fit so precisely that cement was not used. There is one two-storied building, and trapezoidal doors and niches are seen everywhere.

From the solar observatory on the highest part of Machu Picchu, one finds a marvelous panoramic view of the valley. Here is found a stone shaped for use as a sun dial or calendar stone.

Terraces of Machu Picchu

Scholars have dated this magnificent ruin to be somewhere in the late tenth or eleventh century A.D.

Temple of the Sun, Cusco, Peru

CUSCO

Cuzco, the ancient capital of the Incas, is located about 11,000 feet above sea level. One researcher has concluded that it is the oldest continuously inhabited city on the entire American continent. A person can now fly by jet from Lima, Peru, to Cuzco and be met by Indians whose ancestry can be traced back many generations in that one locale. Believed to have been founded in the eleventh century, it was the center of a powerful nation that encompassed Peru, Ecuador, Bolivia, and parts of Argentina. It is also estimated that, by the time of the conquest, Cuzco had over one hundred thousand families.

The Temple of the Sun in Cuzco was the most sacred structure in all of the Inca empire; first built in the twelfth century, it was enlarged several times. Much of the golden treasure that Pizarro took from Cuzco was taken from this temple.

Pictured here is a Catholic church that uses part of the Temple of the Sun as a wall. The curved rocks were placed together without cement and have withstood earthquakes and other damages up to present day—a beautiful example of their engineering skill. Many streets in Cuzco are still lined with walls built by the pre-Columbian peoples. Others who came afterward have built on top of these walls to form the modern buildings that are seen today.

Tambomachay, also known as the "Inca's bath."

Street of Pachacamac

Possible baptismal font or sacred bath of Pachacamac

pachacamac

Temple of the Moon, Pachacamac

Ruins of Pachacamac

The temple and city of Pachacamac are in the Lurin Valley near Lima. A famous location in Inca and pre-Inca times, this area was the scene of the first scientific archaeological work in Peru, under the direction of Dr. Max Uhle. This ruin overlooking the Pacific is believed to have been a pilgrimage center where the pre-Inca creator-god Pachacamac, and later the Inca Viracocha, were worshiped.

Interlocking designs of fish painted in white, yellow, red, and black have been found on the stucco walls. At the Temple of the Sun, northeast of the restored Temple of the Moon, beautiful trapezoidal doors have been painstakingly restored. This temple covers about twelve acres and rises to a height of 75 feet. A large reservoir, aqueducts, and other indications of ancient water systems suggest that irrigation was known and practiced in pre-Columbian times.

At the time of the Spanish Conquest, Pachacamac was a pilgrimage center, the Mecca of Peru. It is with this temple also that the great white god Viracocha is associated.

paracas

Tree of life

The Paracas peninsula lies about eleven miles south of the port of Pisco. Devoid of any vegetation, it is the epitome of loneliness and desolation. Yet in this area is buried the culture that produced some of the best textiles in the world. Some of the textiles were made with as much as 397 threads per inch. The gauges are especially outstanding. Netting, knotting, knitting, twining, plaiting, brocade, weft-patterns, embroidery, and painted cloth were made. Cotton, wool, fibre, and human hair were used in weaving.

The bodies of the Paracas were buried in bottle-shaped chambers at approximately twenty feet. Many were group burials. Many skulls are artificially deformed, and a large portion were trephined.

The Paracas culture existed from approximately 200 B.C. to A.D. 500.

Fortress of Sacsahuaman, Cusco, Peru

sacsahuaman

The great fortress of Sacsahuaman lies above the Cuzco valley. The enormous walls, made from Yucay limestone, stretch for a distance of over 1800 feet. The three terrace walls reach a total height of about 60 feet, with the lowest wall having the largest stones. The largest of these is 27 feet high, 14 feet broad, and 12 feet thick, and weighs an estimated 200 tons.

The area of Sacsahuaman includes buildings, towers, and reservoirs. Transportation of these great blocks of stone required supreme engineering ability. Ropes, manpower, animal power, simple machinery, the principle of the lever, roller, and perhaps the pulley and windlass were used. The massive blocks were fitted together with such excellent precision that there was no need for mortar between, and a thin blade cannot penetrate between the stones. To this day the gigantic stone of Sacsahuaman remains one of the ancient wonders.

It has been conjectured that construction of the fortress of Sacsahuaman, the largest Inca building, required a labor force of 30,000 men.

Possible water filtration plant of Sacsahuaman

The gate of the Sun

tiahuanaco

The highest and most remarkable basin in the Andes is Tiahuanaco, in which lies Lake Titicaca, the highest navigable water in the world, 12,506 feet above sea level. This lake is transversed by a steamboat and has no drainage system except by overflow to Lake Poopo. The basin is divided between Peru and Bolivia, with the great ancient ruins of Tiahuanaco on the Bolivian side. The Aymara Indians make their home here and depend on potatoes, quinoa, and oca for food. This is the homeland of the llama and alpaca.

The center of this culture was probably localized in this area until the early ninth and tenth centuries, when it expanded and spread to the coastal areas. Tiahuanaco itself was a ceremonial center, and the civic organization appears to have been in the hands of a few noble families who inherited their offices through lineage. They understood the processes of irrigation, utilizing canals and other public works.

The major structures of the ruins of Tiahuanaco occupy about a sixth of a square mile on a unique site. No adobe was used; all the ruins are of stone, and there are few walls. The masonry is considered to be the most skillful in Peru. The great monolithic gateway known as the Gateway of the Sun, carved of a single block of andesite, is about ten feet high and twelve and a half feet wide.

The blocks of stone were notched for strength and fitted together by copper clamps, something new in Peruvian masonry. T-shaped grooves were carved into adjacent sides of the rocks, and either copper was pounded into these indentations or molten copper was poured into it and allowed to cool and harden.

These huge basalt and sandstone blocks, weighing up to a hundred tons each, were moved some distance and put into place by these ancient craftsman. The art of polishing, cutting, and clamp-tying these huge stones together is one of the most amazing feats of the world.

Tiahuanaco was also famed for its great human statuary. The largest found so far has been taken to La Paz and erected in a plaza there. The age of this civilization is difficult to determine, but it is thought that the supreme god, Viracocha, created man here.

Guatemalan woman

people and culture

PEOPLES

The Indians of North and South America today represent a cosmopolitan racial group. Indeed, it would be hard to pinpoint a time when they were not. Their origins have been studied by scholars and conclusions are varied. There are strong Old World overtones in the studies of the legends, documents, blood types, facial characteristics, art, and even language.

Today as one travels through Central and South America, except for the very large cities, most of the towns and villages are still "native"—still unchanged, with people living as they have lived for centuries. Progress in the use of modern methods and machinery is very slow, and most of the citizens are very poor. The people are extremely courteous, proud and friendly, yet shy, and very artistic. They love music, and nearly every village has a band that plays for fiestas, where colorful dances are enjoyed. The Castillian citizens of Spanish descent are a separate class, apart from the Indians, and they seldom mix. For the most part, the Spaniards are the civic leaders, while the Indians are the agriculturalists, producing some of the finest fruits and vegetables one will ever see or taste. Those who live near the sea are excellent fishermen; others manufacture many useful items from the maguey plant, such as rope, hammocks, hats, and baskets. Wash day for the country areas is still at the river or community tubs.

Each village has its particular market day, with the local village market still the center of social activity.

The women in the village adorn their bodies with colorful beads as did their ancestors. In Guatemala, especially, there

Guatemalan children

Market place in Guatemala

Drying maguey plant for rope

Guatemalan natives

Natives with their wares

are over 56 different tribes living side by side, yet they seldom mix, each tribe with its own woven fabric, colors, and designs that distinguish it from other tribes. More than half of Guatemala's three million citizens are Indians.

Pottery making is vital, and it is not unusual to see citizens transporting their wares to the market place on their backs, by means of a balance strap held in place on the forehead. Some who are more prosperous have burros.

Religion is very important, and even though Catholicism is the predominant religion, still one observes that many ancient native worship customs are incorporated into the service.

The back-strap loom is an ancient device still very much in use by both women and men, consisting of a belt around the waist with the other end tied to an immovable object. As one travels through the villages, it is not uncommon to see a woman seated outside her hut using her back-strap loom, with the colorful yarns, which she has dyed, hanging on a line nearby.

The economy of Central America is based on agriculture, with coffee and bananas as the chief exports.

It is difficult to speak of the populations of Central and South America as one group, since they are divided into Spanish, Indian, Spanish-Indian mixtures as well as others, including Negroid. Many of the more remote areas have Indians who claim a pure blood line and do not mix with the other groups.

Scenery in the country is spectacular —jutting mountains with lush tropical growth and many lakes. Lake Atitlan in Guatemala is breathtaking in its natural setting of volcanic hills and extremely pleasant weather. South American living for the village citizens is unique in many ways; instead of the burro, the llama is the beast of burden. Known as "the camel of the Andes," this interesting animal is used not only to transport food and wares to market, but when it dies, it is also used for meat, wool, fur, and leather.

There are extremes in altitude in South America. Some peoples live three miles high in the Andes, with much precipitation, while others live at sea level with no more than one inch of rainfall per year.

The ancient spindle whorl is still in evidence; both men and women are seen on the streets and in the fields spinning their yarn in preparation for weaving, as this is, for many, their only means of securing fabric for clothing.

Peruvian farmers still use ancient digging sticks, rakes, and spades, along with the ever-familiar machete and hoes and axes. Their ancient ancestors were known to have domesticated more food and medicinal plants than any other early American groups, and they were quite advanced in their methods of irrigation and storing water. In this agricultural picture, the importance of corn cannot be overemphasized as a staple food for all of Central and South America. It is used as a basis for the tortilla or bread, and Peru raises more varieties than any other area. Almost every home has its little patch of corn, which is dried and stored for future use, and it is surely the bulk of the average diet in this country.

Guatemalan woman

tiahuanaco

The highest and most remarkable basin in the Andes is Tiahuanaco, in which lies Lake Titicaca, the highest navigable water in the world, 12,506 feet above sea level. This lake is transversed by a steamboat and has no drainage system except by overflow to Lake Poopo. The basin is divided between Peru and Bolivia, with the great ancient ruins of Tiahuanaco on the Bolivian side. The Aymara Indians make their home here and depend on potatoes, quinoa, and oca for food. This is the homeland of the llama and alpaca.

The center of this culture was probably localized in this area until the early ninth and tenth centuries, when it expanded and spread to the coastal areas. Tiahuanaco itself was a ceremonial center, and the civic organization appears to have been in the hands of a few noble families who inherited their offices through lineage. They understood the processes of irrigation, utilizing canals and other public works.

The major structures of the ruins of Tiahuanaco occupy about a sixth of a square mile on a unique site. No adobe was used; all the ruins are of stone, and there are few walls. The masonry is considered to be the most skillful in Peru. The great monolithic gateway known as the Gateway of the Sun, carved of a single block of andesite, is about ten feet high and twelve and a half feet wide.

The blocks of stone were notched for strength and fitted together by copper clamps, something new in Peruvian masonry. T-shaped grooves were carved into adjacent sides of the rocks, and either copper was pounded into these indentations or molten copper was poured into it and allowed to cool and harden.

These huge basalt and sandstone blocks, weighing up to a hundred tons each, were moved some distance and put into place by these ancient craftsman. The art of polishing, cutting, and clamp-tying these huge stones together is one of the most amazing feats of the world.

Tiahuanaco was also famed for its great human statuary. The largest found so far has been taken to La Paz and erected in a plaza there. The age of this civilization is difficult to determine, but it is thought that the supreme god, Viracocha, created man here.

metallurgy

It has been observed generally that most of the metallurgy of the ancient Americas consisted of a combination of gold, silver, and copper. The techniques of metallurgy at that time included hammering, embossing, annealing, welding, soldering, strap joining, incising, cut-out designing, and manufacturing bimetallic objects. In Mesoamerica gold was cast by the "lost-wax" or "wax-model" method, and was made into exquisite jewelry.

Iron has been found only in Peru, and there are very few examples. Because of the oxidation property of this metal, few examples indeed would be found if the natives used it in ancient times.

The dainty, exquisite Peruvian gold and silver ornaments include such items as pendants, tweezers, crowns, ear and nose ornaments, cuffs, pins, plaques and discs, earspools, and beads. Some of the gold objects were painted with a colored pigment.

Gold

Atahualpa, the Inca leader, offered to fill a room twenty-five feet long, fifteen feet wide, and nine feet high with gold within sixty days if the Spaniards would release him. Thus he exemplified the availability of gold. The objects that were brought as Atahualpa's ransom were only part of the gold that this empire had gathered. Even now there is perhaps more gold still undiscovered than has been found. It is also thought that the color of gold became sacred to the ancients because it resembled the sun, symbol for their god. They built temples to their sun god and made objects out of gold that resembled the sun.

Scholars believe that gold was not thought of as money or exchange, but was used for ornamental purposes. Sheet gold was used on the inside walls of buildings, and small pieces were sewn on garments for decoration. Animals were sculptured into gold and silver, and these metals were so plentiful that pots, pans, and dishes were made. Even some of their pipes were made of these precious metals. Gilding was done with gold leaf, but the process is not known. Welding was employed at low-heat levels with some kind of chemical mixture.

The gold-copper alloy, tumbaga, became very popular in Colombia, and when hammered it becomes nearly as hard as bronze or soft steel. One of the items that is valued greatly by collectors of ancient artifacts today is the pre-Columbian gold cup—hand wrought, in all sizes and all shapes, and with varying gold content.

According to some authorities, tin and platinum were used as alloys, and bronze was made. Brass has not yet been found. Besides being used for jewelry, these metals were made into blades for digging sticks, mace heads, and lance points.

It is thought that metal working started several hundred years earlier in South America than in Central America.

Gold metalurgy of Peru

Gold cups from Peru

Jewelry

As early as 800 B.C. the Peruvians were masters in the art of fashioning jewelry from turquoise, quartz, lapix luxuli, and other hard stones. Bone, shells, and wood were also used in the creation of such items as beads, pendants, rings, and combs.

Central America's most valuable stone during the Maya civilization was green jade, a semi-precious jewel considered more valuable than gold. Mirrors of silver, copper, and pyrite have been found in ancient burial areas, along with tweezers made of copper, silver, and gold. Inlaid teeth have also been found, as well as ancient hairpins, thorn combs, rings, and costume jewelry in various forms.

The carving was a slow, painstaking process, using crude drills, stone saws, strings, stone, and copper chisels, and rubbing stones with sand as an abrasive.

The ornaments of some of the common people were limited to nose rings and earrings. The more elite had their jewelry made from wax molds.

Gold jewelry of Monte Alban
Gold breast plates from Peru

Portrait jars of South America

pottery

Native Mesoamericans everywhere were adept ceramists. Most of the pottery that has been unearthed appears to be hand modeled by the coil method. The basic pottery shapes are bowls, plates, jars, and bottles. Ceramic decorative techniques included modeling, incising, carving, and painting. Negative painting, an unusual process of decorating pottery, appeared early in Mesoamerica. Items such as whistles, rattles, earplugs, roller and flat stamps or seals, smoking pipes, and spindle whorls were also made.

Among the cultures of ancient Peru, the Mochica civilization produced examples of pottery that were exquisite in their creation of lifelike representations. Dated back to the first six centuries A.D., many of these vessels were undoubtedly modeled after portraits of actual people.

The finest pottery in the Peruvian area is dated between 800 B.C. and A.D. 500. The surface of most of this pottery is black, brown, or red. The most common type was the stirrup-spouted jar; tripod dishes were also used, as well as the common low-level type. Serpents, monkeys, jaguars, and various birds, as well as supernatural beings, were used as subjects for pottery embellishment. Much geometric decoration was also used.

Many examples of the pottery from 300 B.C. to A.D. 500 were made in molds, though duplicates were rare. Humans engaged in many activities are portrayed, together with animals, vegetables, and such objects as houses and boats, erotic scenes, deformations, mutilations, punishments, and captives.

Pottery was a reflection of the pre-Columbian woman; its design was woman-inspired, and the ceramic art should be credited to the proper sex.

Nasca pottery of Peru

Nasca pottery of Peru

Mochica Pottery of Peru

Trepanning

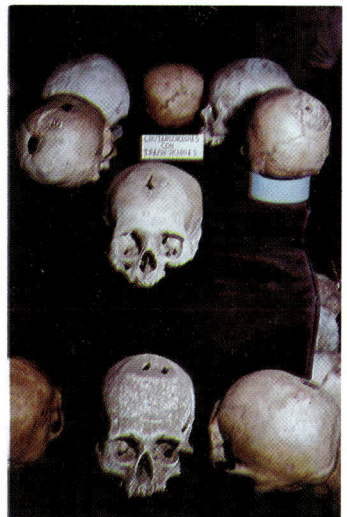
Various Trepanned skulls

Trepanning or trephining involves the removal of a section of the skull to alleviate pressure on the brain or to repair a wound received in battle. This operation was popular anciently in many countries of the eastern Mediterranean world, as well as in the New World.

Surgical instruments used in ancient skull surgery have been unearthed and are now on display in the National Archaeological Museum in Lima, Peru. During a trip to Peru in the 1860s, E. G. Squier uncovered the skull of a Peruvian Indian with a precision-cut, rectangular hole in the left forehead. Since this time, many more skulls having similar holes and dating as far back as 500 B.C. have been unearthed in the Peruvian area. Some of these have silver plates covering the holes. There is every indication that the injury had healed and that the ancient surgery was successful, since the bones had knit together.

Amputation, bone setting, and perhaps even circumcision were practiced by the ancient Peruvians. Various treatments for diseases are indicated, with narcotics used to ease pain. Even white milk from the tree "hoje" was used as a powerful coagulant to stop bleeding.

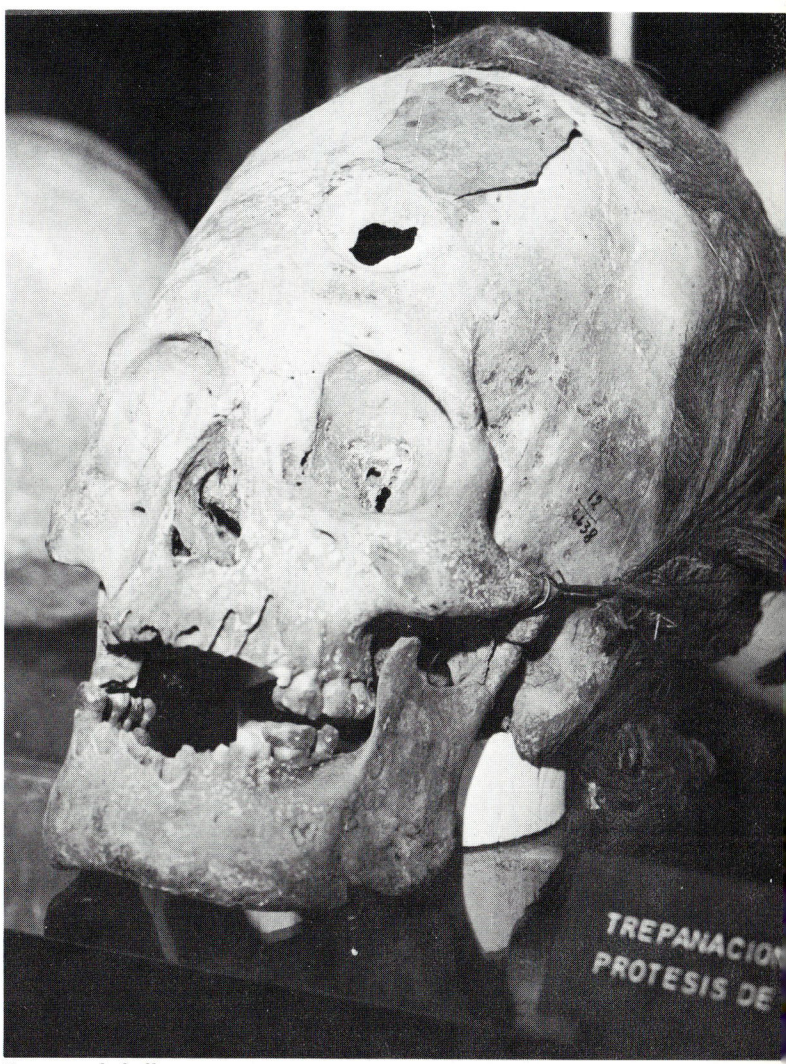
Trepanned skull

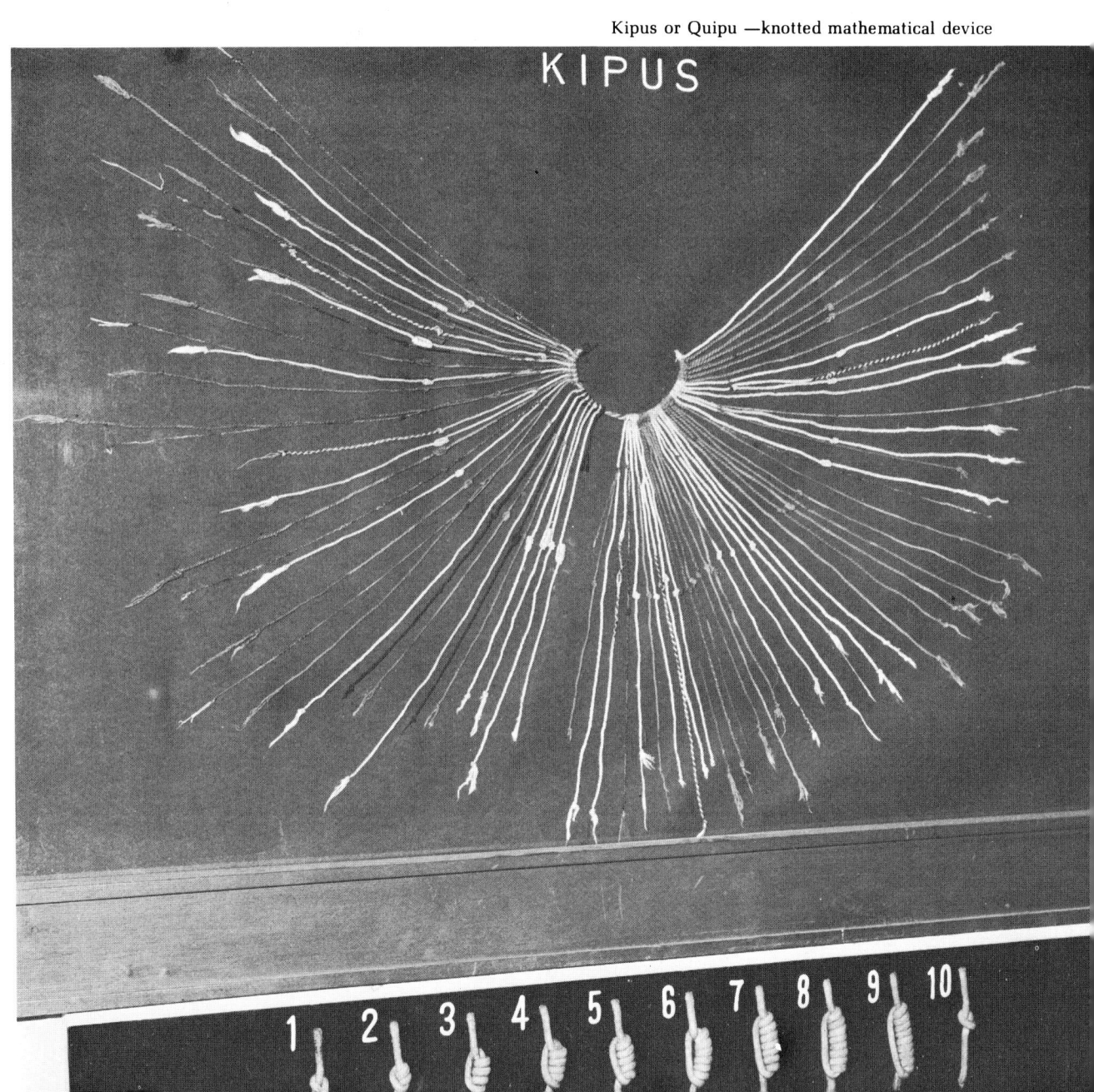

Kipus or Quipu — knotted mathematical device

Quipu

The only "book" in Peru that has been found thus far was a system of knotted cords called *quipu*—a series of knots tied on different colored strings, with the knots varying in size and shape, which constituted the record-keeping system of the ancient Peruvians.

The Inca government kept all of its tax records with a *quipu*, and there was even a symbol for zero. Some scholars believe the use of the zero among the pre-Columbian Indian preceded its use in the Old World.

The number of the knots on the string and the placement of the knots constituted a formula that produced the results. While some would wonder why this is classified as writing, it must be remembered that if messages of mathematical importance were sent from place to place, as was evidently done, this would constitute a form of communication.

It has also been conjectured that the form of the knot and its placement constituted a method of recording names, places, and events. Professional rememberers who knew the meaning of every knot were thought to be employed as interpreters. The *quipu* is an outstanding example of their inventiveness.

Among the Aztec and Mayan Indians, a numbering system of dots and dashes developed. An Indian could dip his hand in paint and use a finger dot for a number and make a stroke for another digit, and combine these for a system of numbering.

Petroglyphs at Newspaper rock, Monticello, Utah

petroglyphs

The fascinating forgotten past of the ancient American inhabitants is written in the rocks of the Americas in the form of petroglyphs, which dot the face of the land from Canada to Mexico and from California to Maine.

Petroglyphs date from the Olmec Culture (800 to 400 B.C.) northeast of Acapulco, Mexico, to post-Columbian times. Dating techniques include the degree of erosion on pigment paintings and the growth of lichens on rocks. The petroglyphs consist of a variety of stick figures, straight and wavy lines, numerous types of animals (birds, deer, the feathered serpent), and the sunburst in a number of designs. Pictoglyphs differ from petroglyphs in that pictoglyphs are drawings or paintings using pigmented compounds, while petroglyphs are scraped or chizzled into the rock surface. Petroglyphs are better preserved than pictoglyphs because they are part of the rock.

Although many symbols and characters are well preserved, no one has succeeded in translating their meaning. A theory has been suggested that perhaps the petroglyphs are symbols used by travelers as a type of trail language. Stick figures pointing in many directions have been found.

Facade of "Nunnery" at Uxmal

106

SUMMARY AND CONCLUSIONS

Three outstanding literary sources aid us in our studies of the early American peoples: (1) the writings of Ixtlilxochitl and other native historians; (2) the records of the early Spanish conquerers and padres; and (3) the Book of Mormon. All three are very valuable, but the Book of Mormon is the most detailed record and was written by men who lived anciently on the American continent. This record, written on metal plates and buried in a stone box, was unearthed in 1823 by a young man named Joseph Smith, who, after much study and preparation, translated these plates into the English language. It covers a history of about 3,000 years in 522 printed pages and is therefore only an abridgment of the actual history. Even though it is not a record of all the pre-Columbian inhabitants of America, still it does provide us with some interesting comparisons with the ancient ruins and artifacts unearthed to date.

Study in the field of archaeology will certainly stimulate one's imagination, as many similarities are found that parallel the Book of Mormon history. This record tells of three groups who migrated to this continent from the Old World near Jerusalem. The Book of Mormon describes large cities with temples, as well as a highly cultured civilization rich in gold, silver, and fine textiles. The record centers around a strongly religious governing body, constantly at war with those who oppose their teachings. Studies of ancient America bear out the fact that there was a highly organized priesthood among the culture, that metallurgy was practiced to a very high degree, and that there was a tremendously developed architectural and agricultural society.

Religion seemed to be the underlying influence among many of the early American groups. The Book of Mormon's central figure of influence is Jesus Christ, whose visits to this continent are recorded therein. All through ancient American legend, and even today in the various tribes on the American continent and the isles of the Pacific, we hear the most enduring legend of all—the story of the bearded white God who came to their ancestors, taught them, blessed them, and promised to return. One cannot help but contemplate on these similarities. There was a fantastic culture here anciently; the Book of Mormon tells of such a society that flowered and died anciently.

In my research on ancient America, along with my study of the Book of Mormon, I have never found anything to dis-

Spring of Tambomachay, Cusco, Peru

courage me in my convictions that the parallels in the two areas are not just coincidental, and yet I have found hundreds of examples that would substantiate the Book of Mormon story.

This pictorial essay is by no stretch of the imagination to be considered as an exhaustive study, but merely a glimpse into the ancient world of the Americas before Columbus.

PRONOUNCIATION GUIDE

Boca Paila — Bokah Píe-lah

Cajamarquilla — Ka-ha-mar-kée-ya
Calakmul — Kah-lahk-móol
Calpullis — Kawl-poo-yées
Caracol — Kaír-ah Kole
Cassava — Kaw-sáw-vah
Chacmool — Chawk-móol
Chayote — Chaw-yóte-ee
Chichen Itza — Chee-chén-eet-sáw
Cholula — Cho-loo-lah
Coatlepantli — Co-awt-lay-pawnt-lee
Codices — Kó-dee-sees
Codz-pop — Kodes-pope
Copan — Ko-pawn
Copilco — Ko-péel-ko
Cuicuilca — Kwee-kwéel-ko

Dzibilchaltun — See-beel-chawl-tóon
El Castillo — el Caw-stée-yo
El Tajin — el Taw-heén
El Salvador — el Sáwl-vah-dore
Etla — até-lah
Guatemala — Gwah-tay-máw-lah
Guerrero — Gyer-ráir-o
Honduras — Hone-duré-aws
Huehuetenango — Whey-whey-tey-nang-go

Itzamna — eet-sáwm-nah
Izapa — Ee-záh-pah
Ixtlilxochitl — Eest-leel-so-chéetl
Kabah — Kah-báw
Kaminaljuyu — Kah-me-nál-hoo-yóo
Kukulcan — Kou-kool-káwn

La Venta — Lah-vén-tah
Labna — Láwb-nah

Maya — Máw-yah
Merida — Mair-ée-dah
Mexico — Mex-ee-ko
Mitla — Meét-lah
Mixteca — Mees-táke-ah
Monte Alban — Moán-tay Awl-báwn

Nicaragua — Neek-ah-ráh-gwa

Oaxaca — Wah-háh-kah
Olmec — Ole-mek

Palenque — Pah-lén-kay
Peten — Pay-tén
Popocatepetl — Pow-pow-cah-táy-petl
Puebla — Poo-éb-lah

Quiche Maya — Kée-chay Máw-yah

Sahagun — Saw-hah-góon

Tehuantepec — Tay-hwán-tay-pek
Tenochtitlan — Tay-noche-teet-láwn
Teotihuacan — Tay-o-tee-hwah-káwn
Tikal — Tee-káwl
Tlachi-hual-tepetl — Tlaw-chee-hwahl-tay-petl
Tlacolula — Tlaw-ko-lóo-lah
Tlatiloko — Tlaw-teel-lolé-ko
Totonac — Tow-tow-náhk
Tula — Tóo-lah
Tzakol — Saw-kóol
Tzintzuntsan — Seen-soon-sáwn

Uxmal — óos-mawl

Verz Cruz — Vair-ah Króos

Xlapak - Slaw-páhk
Xochicalco — So-chee-kall-ko

Guatemalan family

108

Yagul — Yaw-góol
Yucatan — Yoo-kah-táwn

Zaculeu — Saw-koo-lay-oo
Zapotec — Saw-po-tek
Zimatlan — Seem-awt-lawn

GLOSSARY

acropolis — citadel of an ancient city
bichrome — two-color
calendrics — pertaining to the calendar system
caracol — rounded building with a snail construction
caryatid — the figure of a person, usually a woman, which is used as a column to support a roof or ceiling
cassava — same as manioc: a tuberous plant food called tapioca
cenote — well of water
codices — manuscripts of pre-Columbian writing
corbeled — an overlapping of stones, each course projecting beyond the one below
effigy — representation or image especially sculptured
facade — the face of a building
fret — interlaced or angular design
frieze — decorative band or feature on a wall
funerary — pertaining to burial methods
glyph — sculptured symbol
hieroglyph — writing system of symbols that are conventionalized pictures
lichen — plant that grows on rocks
lintel — a horizontal supporting member above an opening such as a window or a door
manioc — tuberous root plant yielding food called tapioca
Mesoamerica — the area of Mexico plus Central America
monolith — single block or piece of stone of considerable size
niche — ornamental recess in a wall
phonetic — speech sound
polychrome — many-colored
portico — a roof supported by columns, usually attached as a porch
potsherd — fragment or broken piece of earthenware
Puuc — range of hills in the Yucatan Peninsula
repousse — raised in relief by pounding on the reverse side
sahagun — Spanish padre who wrote a history of the pre-Spanish Indians
stele — upright pillar of stone bearing an inscription
terra-cotta — hard earthenware of fine quality
trephining — the skull operation wherein part of the bone of the skull is removed
urn — pottery vessel

Gold face mask from Peru